Assembly Lir

GW00102860

Stories, Class-Assemblies, Services and Celebrations for Schools

Written by
Ian MacDonald

Illustrated by
Derry Dillon

First published
September 03 in Great Britain by

Educational Printing Services Limited
Albion Mill, Water Street, Great Harwood, Blackburn BB6 7QR
Telephone: (01254) 882080   Fax: (01254) 882010
e-mail: enquiries@eprint.co.uk   web site: www.eprint.co.uk

ISBN 1 904374 49 2

Acknowledgments

My heartfelt thanks go to all the staff and countless children at the schools I have been privileged to work in. They have provided an appreciative audience for much of the material in this book.

I am grateful also to Nic and Sue for bravely battling against my typing skills in the final editing stage, Mark for rescuing large sections of the book from the hungry jaws of my P.C., and to Linda, at Educational Printing Services Limited, for her ever-cheerful encouragement and advice at the end of the phone-line.

Thank You.

Ian MacDonald M.A. B.Ed.

Scriptures quoted from the anglicised Good News Bible © 1994 published by the Bible Societies / Harper Collins Publishers Ltd., UK. Good News Bible © American Bible Society 1966, 1971, 1976, 1992, 1994. Used with permission.

Songs of Fellowship, ISBN: 0 86065 936 4, 1991, 1992, 1993, published Kingsway Music, Lottbridge Drove, Eastbourne, East Sussex. BN23 6NT.

Come and Praise, 1978, ISBN: 0 563 30444 8, BBC, 35 Marylebone High Street, London, W1M 4AA.

Introduction

An assembly is a strange thing. A colleague once defined this activity as a hymn, a prayer and a rollicking! Some see assembly as an interruption to an already crowded teaching day, others say that they are simply boring (heaven forbid!). However, anyone working in education knows instinctively that the real value of what goes on in school is located in the personal skills, values and attitudes that children (hopefully) acquire in all manner of ways. It is in this aspect of education that the assembly takes centre stage. A really good assembly creates an oasis of reflection, a moment to consider values, those things, which define us as human beings who share a communal planet: truth, goodness, honesty, care, right and wrong. It is a mistake to think that children do not engage in such activity. Given time, and a rollicking good story, they do.

This book provides dramatic assemblies all guaranteed to involve children in actively listening, watching . . . and even taking part. As you will see, Assembly Lines is divided into three sections: The first is packed with a whole range of stories packed in fives to fit neatly into a half term's programme. Each story comes with a simple idea to dramatise the telling for those children who are used to their stories served up on a 14" screen! The second section provides 'off-the-peg' class assemblies with play scripts, poems and presentations...in fact everything you could possibly need for the occasion. Finally, there are five services or celebrations for those special times in the school calendar.

Enjoy!

Ian MacDonald M.A. B.Ed.

CONTENTS _____

PART 2: CLASS LINES
Ten class assemblies complete with presentations, poems, plays, stories etc.
All ready to use, or adapt to suit your own class. 93

PART 3: SERVICE LINES
Complete Services and Celebrations for schools arranged in order as
they occur in a school year. 149

PART 4: RESOURCES
Photocopiable resources to assist with some of the activities
suggested in this book. 177

Assembly Lines

Twenty five stories for assembly each with just a touch of drama!

These stories in this section of the book are organised into sets of five around a central theme, fitting easily into a half term's programme. Each story comes with a simple visual idea to aid the dramatisation of the story, bearing in mind that most children listen better when there is something else to see. The assembly concludes with either a prayer or a reflection. A follow up activity is suggested which may form part of an R.E. or Citizenship lesson, or could well be used where teachers have to provide an assembly in their own classroom.

You'll Never Walk Alone!

STORIES ABOUT HELPING OTHERS

You'll Never Walk Alone!

Theme: Helping Others.

Notes:
The Bible account in Matthew 10 has familiar figures to the Jewish audience of the day, temple officials, a priest and the Samaritan, the most unlikely helper possible. This retelling of the story attempts to remain faithful to the message of the original, while using a setting more familiar to today's children. The chosen teams can easily be interchanged with any arch-rivals closer to your locality.

Preparation:
Bring in a football scarf or similar. An old fashioned supporter's rattle would pose an interesting item for the children to guess its function. Wearing the scarf would signify the setting of this story based on the parable of the Good Samaritan.

The Story:

There was once a man who was returning from the football stadium where he had just watched his team City, play away from home to their arch-rivals United. It had been a hard fought game with several bookings and the usual chanting at the opposing team's supporters. The final score had been 1-1 but, in the last seconds of the game the referee had dismissed shouts for a penalty from the home crowd and many of the United supporters came away grumbling that they had been robbed of three points by a bad decision.

The man, still wearing his blue and white scarf, pushed through the jostling crowds and rounded the corner of the terraced street, feeling inside his coat for his wallet which held his train ticket. The sea of red and white and blue and white was left behind as he cut through a side alley towards the station that would take him to the warmth of his home and a welcome cup of tea. He reached inside his coat for his wallet and checked that his train ticket was still there. Suddenly he felt a sharp blow on the head and he fell to the ground. The man's first reaction was to put his hands over his ears to protect his head and, as he did so a hand reached down and roughly tore open his jacket. Just as quickly the hand removed the wallet from the supporter's pocket and he felt something thud into the side of his head as the three youths ran off down the road.

4

The man put his hand to his forehead and found a small trickle of blood. He tried to stand up but he found that his ankle hurt badly and he was unable to move except to struggle into a sitting position and lean against the fence. In a few moments it became quiet, the chatter and shouts of the returning football supporters disappeared, and the man was left alone.

Minutes became half an hour, and then an hour and, just when the man had begun to give up hope of being spotted, he heard the sound of approaching footsteps. As he looked up he saw a woman stop at the end of the alleyway. She wore a blue and white scarf the same as he did. Hopefully the man sat forward and waved to show that he needed help. The new arrival looked down the alleyway and then glanced nervously over her shoulder. Hesitating for only a moment the supporter disappeared back the way she had come and all was quiet again. The man slumped back against the fence. She must have been afraid of being attacked too thought the man.

It was dark now and the alleyway was lit only by the light of a dim street lamp. The man pulled his torn coat around him to keep out the cold. For the second time that day he heard the sound of footsteps. Looking up he saw another figure appear at the entrance to the alleyway. The supporter strained his eyes to see. There, sure enough, lit for a moment by the lamp was the match referee. He could see the badge on the man's jacket, he carried a sports bag and a small black whistle could still be seen about his neck. The referee paused, looked hard at the man on the ground, and then he too returned the way he had come.

"I shall never be found," groaned the poor supporter on the hard ground. "I shall be here all night and will catch a terrible cold, or worse." Now even the sound of the traffic had grown quiet and the man knew that it was getting late.

Then, for a third time came the sound of someone approaching. The supporter looked up hopefully but his heart sank when he saw that, walking towards him was a youth wearing the red and white of UNITED.

"Oh No!" groaned the City supporter, "Now I'm really in trouble."

The youth came nearer and nearer and stopped. He bent down.

"What is the matter?" asked the United fan. And with the gentlest touch he sat the man forward and looked at his wounds. Taking his red scarf he made a bandage about the man's forehead and he lifted him to his feet. Then, step by step, he carried the man along the passage way until they reached the station. He took some money from his own wallet and bought a train ticket for the man and put him safely on the train. In less than an hour the man was safe at home.

And, if you should ever call to visit, you will see two scarves hanging on the supporter's bedroom wall. The blue of City and the red of United.

Prayer:

Dear God,
Help us to help others. May we not be like those who walked by without caring. May we help others whether they appear to be like us or very different from us, whether they are black or white, rich or poor, girl or boy.
Amen.

Follow Up:

What things stop us from helping others, their appearance, our own feelings, fear etc.? Think of practical ways we might help others. Is it appropriate to put ourselves in danger to help someone else? (for example, diving into the sea to rescue someone!)

What's Cooking?

Theme: Treating others fairly.

Notes:
In this traditional Muslim tale children will easily identify how unfairly the restaurant owner behaves. They will enjoy the solution to the story and can consider the times when they use the phrase 'It's not fair!' The central character in the story is Nasrudin the Mullah (teacher) who is a recognised folk hero across the Muslim world. Here he shows his great wisdom.

Preparation:
You will need a few coins in your pocket, or in a cloth purse that can be rattled at the appropriate moment for dramatic effect. A piece of paper will represent the bill that the restaurant owner brandishes at Raoul.

The Story:

Raoul the beggar sat in his place in the street of a thousand houses. He had no money and the few scraps of food he gleaned from passers by just about kept the skin on his old bones. Nevertheless, Raoul was not a miserable character and he always had a smile to spare for those who found the time to wish him good morning, or drop a penny in his begging bowl, on the way to market.

On this particular morning Raoul sat in his usual spot close by to the market place knowing that, amongst the bustle of shoppers, there would be some who would stop for a moment to find a coin in their purse or spare some food from their shopping basket. He was enjoying the warmth of the sun on his face when something caught his attention. From a nearby doorway came the most delicious aroma of cooking. He lifted his face to catch the full flavour of the variety of smells that tantalised his nostrils. He sniffed at the air and closed his eyes.

"Mmmm!" He could almost see the white plates, the juicy meats, the steaming vegetables, the colourful spices and rich sauces. And the smell was coming from over there.

He stood up and walked to the building the smell seemed to be coming from.

Raoul found himself standing in the entrance to a fine restaurant. Inside were white tablecloths, customers seated at tables in their fine clothes, and, on every table were delicious looking plates of steaming, hot dinners.

"How I wish that I could go inside and eat," sighed the old beggar, "but I shall be content for today to simply enjoy the smell of this fine cooking." He lifted his face to the heavens again and almost drank in the delicious aroma as he breathed in deeply.

Suddenly Abu Bakr, the owner of the restaurant, appeared from inside.

"Just what do you think you are doing sniffing the air outside my restaurant?" he demanded.

"I am sorry," began the beggar, "but I did not think that I was doing any harm. Surely you cannot begrudge me the smell of your food."

"But you are putting my customers off their dinner!" said the owner. "Get yourself away from my establishment this instant."

Poor Raoul shuffled away and returned to his place in the market. But, as the afternoon wore on, and he had nothing to eat, he could not resist returning to Abu Bakr's restaurant for one last sniff.

Just as was taking in the rich aroma of cooking Abu Bakr appeared again. He was furious.

"I told you that I did not ever want to see you here again," he shouted. "You will have to pay for what you have done."

"But I have done nothing," replied the beggar. "I have only smelled your food."

"Then here is the bill," said the owner, thrusting a piece of paper under the man's nose. "The bill for smelling my food is the amount written here."

The old man's eyes widened. "I cannot pay you this. I have no money."

"Then you shall meet me at court in the morning," said Abu Bakr, and with that he stormed back into his restaurant.

Standing nearby was Nasrudin the Mullah (a mullah is a teacher). He had heard everything. He went up to Raoul and said, "Do not worry. I have heard what has been spoken here. I shall be at the court tomorrow to help you. Good day to you, Raoul."

All that night as the beggar pulled his cloak about him against the cold of the night, he could not sleep for fear of what was to happen the next day.

Morning came and Raoul stirred himself and made his way to the court room. When he arrived Abu Bakr was there before him. The old beggar shuffled sadly to his place.

"What is the case to be heard," said the judge, a great man seated at a large wooden desk.

"The case my Lord, is that this beggar here has smelled my food and must pay the bill that I hold in my hand."

"My Lord," said a voice. It was Nasrudin the Mullah. "May I speak for the accused?"

The judge, recognising Nasrudin, nodded for him to continue.

"I would like to pay the bill for this man, if you will allow it."

Everyone looked and waited to see what would happen next.

From out of his coat pocket the Mullah took a small purse of coins. He walked to the restaurant owner and shook it by his ear.

"There you are. The payment for smelling your dinner…the sound of my money."

The judge smiled. Everyone in the court began to laugh and the case was settled.

Reflection:

"That's not fair!" We all recognised that Abu Bakr had treated Raoul unfairly. How quick are we to say 'It's not fair'? Do we accept when things are fair, although they may not always go in our favour? Let's take a moment to think whether we act fairly to others.

Follow Up:

In the circle share a time when you felt that something was unfair. Let others in the circle comment on whether each circumstance was unfair to everyone involved. Is it possible to be fair to everyone all the time?

The Hospital Picture

Theme: People who help us.

Preparation:
Bring in some simple items that could be associated with a hospital: bandages, plasters, a thermometer etc. You may even be able to borrow a stethoscope or a doctor's white coat, although avoid anything at all alarming! Ask the children who might use these things. Tell the children that today's story is about a child who had to undergo an operation on her leg.

The Story:

All along the floor of the corridor there were different coloured lines, like the lines on roads that stopped you parking. They reminded Ellie of the road that day when she had tripped at the kerb. Luckily there had not been any cars coming but she had badly twisted her knee and now she was going to have an operation. The nurse walked down the corridor beside her and chatted to her along the way.

"My name's Marion," said the nurse. "When we get to the theatre I will be there all the time and I will be there when you wake up from your operation."

"But I don't feel sleepy," said Ellie.

"No, I'm sure you don't," smiled Marion, "but the doctor will give you something to make you go to sleep, and when you wake up your leg will have been mended."

"Will I be able to go running and do my skipping?" asked Ellie.

"Not straight away," said the nurse, "but in time you will, when you have had time to recover."

Now the lines on the floor had changed from red to green and in front of them were two doors. Ellie and Marion went inside and there was a man wearing gloves and a green mask over his mouth. He pulled down his mask for a moment to smile and say hello to Ellie. The nurse helped Ellie onto a bed with wheels on and she explained that this was to bring her back to her bed later. Another nurse came in and smiled too. All these people seemed very nice, but all the same, Ellie wished that she was at home watching her favourite television programme, instead of being in this room with the bright lights and strange instruments on the walls.

On one wall was a picture and Ellie let her eyes wander over the scene? There was a lake in the centre of the picture and behind the lake were several misty, grey hills in the distance; a group of sheep were grazing nearby. But what caught Ellie's attention the most was in the foreground of the painting, there, crouching low on a rock was a black collie-dog and standing in front of the dog was the smallest baby lamb. Ellie thought that the dog looked like he might pounce on the lamb, or was about to bark and frighten it. Ellie thought that the lamb should be with the other sheep and not anywhere near this nasty dog.

"I'm just going to put a little medicine in your arm, Ellie," said the man in the green mask, "you will feel a little tingle in your arm, and then you will go to sleep for a while."

Ellie did not want to have the needle in her arm; nor did she want to go to sleep. She did not want to be here with these people. She looked at the picture on the wall. There were the mountains, the lake and the sheep; but she could no longer see the dog and the tiny lamb. Ellie felt her eyes grow heavy but she wanted to look again at the picture. She wanted to see where the lamb and the dog had gone.

And then she found herself by the lake and she was dipping her hand in the cool water and brushing it onto her forehead. The grass under her feet was green and soft and at the waters edge reeds were bending gently in the breeze. Looking up she saw a flock of birds soaring over the mountains and nearby several sheep were munching lazily at the grass. But nowhere could she see the lamb or the black dog.

Ellie was determined to find out where they had gone. She set off across the grassy meadow towards the hills. As she went the breeze from the lake began to grow cold and she was surprised to see that she was wearing her blue dressing gown as she pulled the warm material about her shoulders.

Now she had begun to climb the rocky layers at the foot of the hills and a little stream babbled and sang as it made its way down over pebbles and boulders. But there was no sign of the lamb here. Ellie climbed higher still, her slippers barely offering protection against the sharp rocks under her feet. It was then that she heard the faint sound. At first she thought it was only the sound of the wind whistling through the branches of the trees but, as she listened harder she was sure that she could make out the faint bleating of a sheep…or even a lamb. Higher and faster she climbed until she came to a rocky outcrop of stone, and peering over the edge, she could see, some feet below her, the tiny lamb. It looked up at her and bleated once. Ellie guessed that it had fallen and could not climb back up the steep slope. Ellie looked about her for something with which she might reach the stranded creature. She could see nothing.

Then, just as she was about to clamber over the edge, and risk tearing her new pyjamas, she heard another sound. It was the dog. It appeared from behind the little girl and, ignoring her, it scrambled down to where the lamb was.

"Oh No!" thought Ellie. "Surely the dog will frighten the lamb and it will fall."

But, as she watched, fascinated, the dog circled behind the lamb and crouched low and silent, just as Ellie had remembered seeing it before, in the picture. The black collie dog gave three short sharp barks and inched forward and then stopped again. As it did so the lamb backed and turned and then Ellie could see the narrow pathway that she had not seen before, hidden almost by a small yellow bush to one side of the ledge. Slowly, but carefully the dog steered the lamb along the ledge until it disappeared from Ellie's view, and then it appeared again behind her and she watched as the two creatures almost skipped and ran down the mountain slope. Ellie stood up but she could not run and her head felt slightly dizzy.

"Ellie, Ellie, wake up. It's all done."

There was Marion bending over her, and her mum too. "The operation's all done and you'll soon be up and about again."

"Look," said the nurse. "I've swapped this picture for the one in the theatre that you seemed to be looking at when you went to sleep."

Ellie looked. There was the dog crouching again by the lamb. Now she realised that the dog was not going to harm the lamb, but that it was gently guiding it back to the safety of the rest of the flock. She realised too that the lamb might be afraid of the dog because she did not understand what it was doing.

She remembered what she had thought about the doctors before she had gone to sleep in the operating theatre. She had not wanted them to put the needle in her arm and send her to sleep. She had wanted them to leave her alone. She thought again about the lamb and felt that she knew just how it must have felt when the dog came and barked at it. But Ellie now knew that the doctors, just like the dog in the picture, were doing it for her good.

Prayer:

Dear God,

Help us to be grateful for all those who help us even when we do not realise it. When our parents tell us off for doing wrong things, when someone gives us medicine we do not like or when a friend may tell us something we do not want to hear. Help us to appreciate that these things may be for our own good.

Help us to find the grace to say thank you even when we do not feel like it.
Amen.

Follow up:

Talk about people who help us. Do we always realise when people are doing something for our good? Should adults be allowed to make decisions for children? What kind of decisions should children make for themselves?

The Crested Bird and The Snake

Based on a traditional story from the West Indies

Theme: Working together.

Preparation: *None.*

The Story:

The men who made their homes on earth in the rich forests and jungle of Guyana divided themselves into tribes. Some settled on the good land and planted crops and fed the children from what they grew. Some journeyed to the far places where the purple mountains seemed to shake hands with the sky. But where every man slept, there he made a shelter for himself from the sun and the rain. Each tribe had its own leader who saw that each one was looked after and that everyone had their place.

But the animals who watched the men from the forest had no one to lead them. Because they had no leader the animals often fought among themselves for food, or argued and squabbled about who should live where in the forest. One day, tired of the constant disputes the animals called a meeting in the place where the trees had not grown.

As soon as the animals met together they began to put their case to convince the others that they would be the most suited to be the leader.

"I should be the leader for I am quick and nimble and can climb higher than anyone," said Irraweka the brown monkey.

"I am the best animal for the job because I know how to find food on the forest floor," said Mapuri the pig.

A parrot squawked that she had the most colourful plumage; a jaguar boasted that he could run faster than any, and the buffalo said that he was the natural leader because of his size alone.

After an age of arguing a voice cut into the noise. It was the wise owl.

"If you want a leader look there to that tree. See the Powis Bird. He will lead you well."

"No, no," spluttered the Powis Bird, "I cannot be your leader. I do not

1 4

have a fine strong voice nor bright colourful plumage like the parrot. Choose someone else."

But everyone agreed that the Powis Bird, who said little but thought much, would be a great leader and so it was that he was chosen. And to crown him, the animals collected together fine feathers from the forest birds and fashioned them to make a crest for their King.

No sooner had this been done than disaster struck. While the Powis Bird and his mate were searching together for berries for their dinner a snake crept out of the undergrowth, into the bird's nest, and wrapped itself around the two white eggs that were not long for hatching.

"Oh no!" cried Powis Bird's mate when she arrived back. "My chicks are soon to hatch and they will be eaten by the snake who is waiting for his lunch."

The Powis Bird called together the animals from the forest to come to his aid. They were anxious to help their leader and again began to boast which of them would be able to rescue the eggs.

"I could jump on the snake's back and destroy him," shouted Mapuri, the pig.

"But that would upset the nest and send it tumbling to the forest floor," wailed the female bird.

"I could pierce the snake with my sharp horns," said the cow.

"But the snake will spring up in pain and knock the eggs to the ground," said the Powis Bird.

"I could roar to frighten the snake away," said the jaguar.

"But the noise will shake the eggs so that they will crack and the chicks will not hatch."

Other animals offered, the buffalo, the monkey, the sloth and many others but no one had a plan that would satisfy the King and his wife.

"You have one creature you have not asked," said the owl. "Go and ask the ant."

"But he is so small. He will be of no use at all," cried the other animals.

"He is so small that the snake will not notice him, and he will go on sleeping," laughed the hyena.

But no one had a better idea and so the ant was sent for. He wasted no time in scuttling into the nest. There he stung the snake sharply on its tail. The snake opened one eye and blinked. And then another ant appeared and another, until there were a thousand ants all biting the snake with their sharp stings.

As the Powis Bird and the other animals watched, the snake uncoiled itself and slithered along the tree branch and away along the forest floor. And that is how the tiny ant proved that one little creature working together with his friends can achieve something good.

Prayer:

Help us Lord God to appreciate the importance of each person here in this room today. May we learn that, each playing our part, we can do something together to make our world a better place.
Amen.

Follow Up:

Put a table and building bricks, preferably interlocking such as Lego, into the middle of the circle. Stand one brick up and ask someone to knock it over with one little finger. Give everyone a brick and build a wall. See if the same person can easily break the wall down from its end with one finger. Talk about things we can do together that we are less likely to achieve alone.

Billy's Face

Theme: Playing our part.

Preparation:
Have a picture of a face in bits i.e. nose, mouth, eyes etc. This might be a manufactured version, or one you have quickly made with paper, the parts ready prepared with double-sided tape or similar. Ask two children to put the face together at a board, one blindfolded, and the other giving instructions. When complete comment on the importance of the right bits in the right place doing the right job. What would it be like if you had forgotten to put the nose on etc. This is the subject of today's story.

The Story:

Billy's face decided not to behave. It was all very inconvenient.

The day had started badly anyway. Billy was getting a hard time from several of his friends about sports day. He did not want to be in the relay and they were one short.

"But we need someone to run the last leg," said Amy.

"Why don't you use your own leg?" replied Billy, shuffling his feet on the ground.

"Ha, ha, very funny," said Tom, "you know what Amy means, "we need someone to run the last bit of the race and you could do it."

"I could, but I really don't want to," Billy went on. "I'm not the fastest runner in the school."

"No, maybe not but with all of us together we might not be that bad," said Jo, "and, anyway, we can't enter without four people, it's not allowed."

That night Billy had trouble getting off to sleep. He could not stop thinking about his friends going on at him. He wished that they would just leave him alone. It was then that his face went bonkers!

It was his nose that went first. It just up and went, walked right off the place between where his eyebrows stopped and his mouth began.

"Well that's charming!" said Billy's mouth. "Who does he think he is, going off like that? Does he think we like it stuck here on this boy all day?"

"What do you know about it?" replied one of Billy's eyes. "You can't talk."

"I can actually," said Mouth.

"I mean," went on the Eye, "that you can't talk, you're only interested in yourself and what you've got to say."

"Well if you're asking me to see things your way, then you've got another think coming."

"Thinking! - that's a good one," joined in one of the eyebrows. "I thought that was Brain's job."

"Why don't you mind your own business," sneered Mouth. "Just concentrate on going on a head. On ahead, get it?"

"Well we're all doing that aren't we?" said the eyebrow. "If it wasn't for Billy's head we wouldn't be here at all."

"Well perhaps Nose has got the right idea. Perhaps he thinks he can do alright for himself on his own. And why shouldn't he? See you around," said Eye, and with that he hopped off the face, bounced once on the table, and skipped out of the door.

Once out in the fresh air Eye bounced along merrily enjoying all the things he could see. He passed fields and cows and trees and boats on the river. Everything was so colourful. Everything was so green and bright and was as if it was all there just for him to see and enjoy.

"I don't know why I didn't try this before," thought Eye to himself. "I don't need all those others. Mouth was always mouthing off and Nose was always very stuck up. They both thought they were the most important. I am far better than either of them, I can see."

Very soon he came to a town. The town was very large and everywhere Eye looked he saw streets, shops, houses and office blocks. There were people and cars everywhere. Just as he was about to cross the road who should he bump into but Nose.

"I see you've escaped as well," sniffed Nose. "You had to copy my idea I suppose."

"I had been thinking about it myself for sometime," blinked Eye.

"Well I don't need you to see I'm alright," said Nose and walked off with his nose (which was all of him) held high in the air. Stepping off the curb he began to cross the road. If he had been an eye he would have seen the lorry coming. If he had been an ear he might have heard it. But he was not. And Eye looked away as poor Nose was the victim of a hit and run accident.

Eye blinked. He had seen it all. "Why didn't he watch where he was going?" he said to himself and he began to retrace his steps, or rather his bounces, in the way he thought he had come. Unfortunately his nose for direction was not very good. Neither did he smell the chemical factory, nor did he hear the sound of the strange puddle of liquid that bubbled at the roadside, spilt from a passing tanker only five minutes before. It wasn't long before Eye had stumbled into the deadly puddle and had come to a sticky end. And that was when Billy sat up. He rubbed his eyes and blinked. Yes, they were both there. He ran his hands along his nose and mouth in turn and put his fingers gingerly into his ears. His face was all present and correct.

"So will you run the race or not?" asked Jo when she met Billy on the playground.

"Yes," replied Billy at once.

"What's changed your mind?"

"You don't want to know," muttered Billy. "Something someone said about all doing our bit, I think."

Jo gave him a puzzled look and ran off to tell her friends the good news. Later that day, as Mr Jenkins clicked his stopwatch at the end of the relay he confirmed the result.

"Billy's team...BY A NOSE!"

Bible Reading:

I Corinthians 12 v 14-18 (the Good News Bible)

"Now the body itself is not made up of one part but of many. If the foot should say to the hand, "because I am not a hand I do not belong to the body," that would not keep it from being part of the body. And if the ear were to say, "because I am not an eye I do not belong to the body," that would not keep it from being part of the body. If the whole body was just an eye, how could it hear? And if it were an ear, how could it smell? As it is, however, God has put every different part in the body just as he wanted it to be."

Prayer:

Dear God,

May each of us realise that we are stronger together than we are alone. Help us to play our part in our families, among our friends and in this community at school, so that together, we become the best that we can be.
Amen.

Follow Up:

Give everyone in the circle a piece of paper with the name of someone in the group/class. Finish this sentence on the paper " . . . . is a valuable person in this group/class because…" The teacher may need to give an example e.g. "because she says kind things about people." Do not allow anyone to opt out. Shuffle and read out.

Unlikely Heroes

TRUE STORIES OF ORDINARY PEOPLE WHO DID EXTRAORDINARY THINGS

Pickles

The true story of the little dog who found the World Cup

Theme: We can all do something special.

Preparation:

Ask the children who their heroes are. The chances are that they will suggest pop-stars, super-heroes like Batman, soldiers or famous footballers. You might tell them that this set of stories tells of those who are unlikely heroes...but who, nevertheless, did something very special.

The Story:

Every football fan knows the names of some of the great heroes of the World Cup: Ronaldo, Figo, Pele, David Beckham. Some even remember the great England team of 1966, who won the World Cup at Wembley Stadium: Bobby Charlton, Gordon Banks, Captain Bobby Moore and little Nobby Stiles who danced a jig all the way around the stadium. But few remember the name of another World Cup Hero of that famous year. His name was Pickles.

Pickles was an unlikely hero. He would not have been picked for any football team. He was far too small! But without him England could not have lifted the World Cup on that special day in July. All the more surprising because Pickles was no more than a little black and white dog.

His story began in the spring of 1966, when preparations were being made to hold the most famous football event in the world, in England. All the greatest football stadiums were going to be used, and Wembley Stadium would hold the cup-final itself. Tickets were printed and travel companies were preparing to receive thousands of football fans from all over the world. Even the beautiful Jules Rimet Trophy, the prize for the winning team in July, had been specially flown to London ready for the start of the great tournament. It had been polished and placed carefully in a glass case in Westminster Hall, where eager crowds queued to see it.

"Look at that Dad," said a small boy, as he pressed his nose to the glass.

"That's the Jules Rimet Trophy, that is, son," said his Dad. "It's the greatest prize in football, and we're hoping our lads are going to win it."

"Are they going to Dad?"

"Course we will," said the boy's Dad, "we've got Bobby Charlton, and his brother Jack, and then there's the West Ham lads, Peters, Bobby Moore, and that new boy, Geoff Hurst."

As the people filed past they admired the golden winged statue on the tiny cup. It did not seem possible that the trophy, estimated to be worth £30,000, was in London and that the best teams in the world would soon be playing for it in stadiums all over the country.

Then disaster struck. One day, in broad daylight, the trophy was stolen, right from under the noses of the security guards. A message was sent to the Chairman of the Football Association asking for a huge ransom to be paid to the thief who had stolen the trophy. Along with the message was a package wrapped in newspaper. It was the top of the cup, just to prove that the thief really did have the cup in his possession.

"Just look at this, love." Dave Corbett sat back from the table and thumbed at an article in the paper. His wife Jean leant across the table, a cup of tea still warm in her hand.

"What is it?" she asked.

"It's the World Cup, look," Dave went on. "You know, that was stolen from the exhibition in London."

"Yes, I remember," said his wife.

"Well, that bloke, the one the boys in blue were looking for, they've got 'im."

"Well I never," said his wife, "and what about the cup. Have they got that back too?"

"No, it seems it's still missing."

"You can't have a World Cup competition without a cup to win, can you?"

"No, I suppose not. There's a reward though, for helping the police to get it back. Six thousand quid!"

"Six thousand pounds? That would be nice. I could do with a holiday."

Dave laughed, put down his paper, and picked up a brown, leather lead. "Come on boy. Come on Pickles, time for your walk."

A little black and white dog pricked up his ears and followed his master to the door.

Dave Corbett lived in London, and he worked alongside the River Thames. There was nothing he liked better than a stroll along the river with Pickles trotting along at his side. Today was a bright spring morning and the street lights were just beginning to go off. The traffic was not yet busy; it was too early. A few men in suits hurried to work to beat the morning rush. The dustmen were emptying bins into the back of a cart. Pickles chased a newspaper wrapper that blew along in the breeze from the river.

"Come on Pickles," laughed Dave, "you won't find anything in there."

But Pickles could smell the fish and chips that had been in there the night before. If there was anything going, Pickles would find it!

In a few moments they would be at the park and Pickles would have a good run around, perhaps chase a few pigeons, or even a cat! The street on which they were walking was quieter than the busy main street, and Pickles was straining at the leash. He could see the black railings of the park in the distance and was keen to get there.

"Go on then, boy," said Dave, and he bent down and let the little dog off the lead.

He padded on ahead, just keeping his master in range, but never letting his eye off the park gate ahead. But then, without any warning, Pickles suddenly vanished into the bushes at the side of the pavement.

"What's up boy?" said Dave, and he broke into a trot.

When he arrived Pickles was frantically pulling at some newspaper under the dark hedge.

"Come on boy, there's nothing in those newspapers. I told you before."

But Pickles took no notice. He wrestled the newspaper out on to the pavement.

"What is it boy?" said Dave. "What have you got there Pickles?"

Dave bent down and from the paper he drew a small, gleaming statue. "Well, blow me down. It's the World Cup."

It was now July and Pickles sat at his master's feet as the black and white pictures flickered on the little television set.

"Hurst has the ball and he's heading into the German half with the score at 3-2 to England. Some people are on the pitch . . . they think it's all over. . ."

There was a roar from the crowd as Geoff Hurst rifled in the fourth goal. 4-2 to England! The commentator's voice could just be heard above the cheering . . .

"It is now!"

Dave threw his arms up in the air and joined in the celebration. England had won the cup.

Pickles cocked his head to one side, not sure what all the fuss was about. He just wanted to go for his walk to the park. After all; you just never know what you might find?

Prayer:

Dear God,

Help us to remember that great things have been achieved by ordinary people. Help us to realise that we too might do something special today, in our work, or in what we say, or in helping someone who is in need.
Amen.

Follow up:

Find out about other unsung heroes. Who is your hero? It might be a member of your family, a friend, someone you admire. What are the qualities in a person that makes them a hero? Write about your personal hero and draw their picture.

Mary Jones' Bible

The true story of the little girl who wanted her own Bible

Theme: Perseverance.

Preparation:
Bring in a selection of Bibles. Ask the children if they can remember wanting something really badly. What would they have been prepared to do to own it? The little girl in today's story wanted a Bible of her own. She was prepared to go to great lengths to get it.

The Story:

Mary Jones banged the shirt against the wet boulder that sat, half in half out of the stream that trickled and babbled down the mountainside. Mary was doing the washing in the days before washing machines had been invented. It was not even her washing. She was washing clothes for other people to pay for the one thing she wanted more than anything: her own Bible.

Mary Jones lived with her mother in the little village of Llanfihangely, in Wales. They did not have very much and could not afford to buy nice things or expensive clothes to wear. Her mother could barely afford the shoes to put on her daughter's feet. Their one outing of the week was to walk to the church on a Sunday to hear stories read from the Bible in their own Welsh language. Mary loved to hear the stories of Jesus, or the story of Noah's ark, or Jonah being swallowed by a whale. When Mary was eight years old a school opened for the first time in the village. Now Mary had the chance to learn to read. It was an hour's walk to the new school every day, but Mary did not complain.

"One day," she thought, "I shall be able to read my very own Bible." At first she could not understand the strange squiggles and marks in the books that were put in front of her. But Mary was a very determined girl and, bit by bit, she began to make sense of the words on the page. In time she had learned to read the simple books that the school provided and, on Saturdays, Mary was lucky enough to be able to visit Mrs Evans who had a Bible in the Welsh language, and was willing to allow Mary to come to read it for herself. But learning to read was only the first step.

Now Mary had the idea of doing jobs for other people to save enough to buy herself a Welsh Bible. She began by doing the washing down at the stream; she knitted socks, weeded flower beds and looked after younger children. When Mrs Evans got to hear about Mary's hard work she gave Mary some baby chicks to look after. When they grew to adult hens Mary was able to sell the eggs and put the money into her savings. Each time she was paid a few pennies she counted them each night to see how close she was to buying her precious Bible.

After six whole years of saving hard Mary finally had enough money. There was nowhere in the village that sold Bibles. The nearest Bible shop was in Bala, twenty five miles away. Not put off by the distance, Mary set off with just the clothes she was wearing and a tiny purse of money clutched tightly in her hand.

At first the journey seemed pleasant. The sun shone, and Mary walked in the shadow of Cader Idris, the great mountain which was to keep her company most of the way. On the way she passed a flock of sheep lazily munching on some grass by the side of the road.

"Hello, sheep. I'm off to Bala to buy my first Bible."

Baa! Bala? Baa! Bala? The sheep appeared to reply.

A little later Mary had to leave the road way and begin to climb the slopes of the mountainside. She stopped for a rest by the brook and dabbled her feet in the water for a moment. She looked down at her precious shoes. They were already dusty and any shine had disappeared.

"Mother has saved her pennies, just as I have saved mine, so that I can have these shoes to wear, and now I'm going to spoil them," thought Mary. And with that she put the shoes in her spare hand and set off bare foot across the next field.

Hours past and still Mary walked and walked. Her step no longer had its spring and even the money in her purse seemed to grow heavy. The sky darkened with the approach of the late afternoon. The fifteen year old began to wonder if she had come the right way. Mary sat down on a grassy bank exhausted. She could go no further. It was then that she saw, in the distance, the grey point of a church spire. It was Bala. Mary's feet were sore, and her head ached, but she set off again, and in another hour she stood outside the shop of Reverend Charles. Mary had been walking for twenty five hours.

At the shop the Reverend looked up and recognised Mary from the Bible reading in Llanfihangely. "What are you doing here, Mary?" he asked, glancing down at her muddy feet.

"I've come for a Bible," said Mary as she opened her purse, letting the pennies spill onto the shop counter.

Reverend Charles looked at the coins and then the young girl who smiled up at him.

"Oh, Mary," he said, "its true that we have some Bibles here printed in the Welsh language, but everyone has been in to buy them. There is only one left, and it is already promised to someone in the town. They are coming to pick it up in the morning."

Mary could not help the tears. They trickled down her face and she began to pick up her coins and put them back in her purse. All that way for nothing. She turned away and opened the door.

"Wait!" The Reverend Charles put a hand on Mary's shoulder. "Come back inside Mary. I have promised the Bible to someone, but they can wait. When they hear of the trouble you have been to to get this Bible I am sure that they won't mind waiting a bit longer."

And that is how Mary Jones got her very own Bible.

As a result of Mary's incredible story, The British and Foreign Bible Society was formed to make it possible for people across the world to read the Bible in their own language.

Prayer:

Dear God,

We thank you for the story of Mary Jones and her Bible. May we learn to keep trying when things become difficult; and not give up. Amen.

Follow Up:

Look at different versions of the Bible. Compare the different language used (modern, old-fashioned etc.) Which ones are easier to understand? Find out about the work of organisations such as The Bible Society.

A Final Friendship

The Legend of St Alban

Theme: Sacrifice.

Preparation:

This story can be easily dramatised to spring a surprise on the audience, tricking the onlookers in the way that the Roman soldiers were hoodwinked. It is very easy to set up. You will need two children of similar height and appearance; two large pieces of material enough to cloak the two from head to foot (red for Alban, brown for the monk); and a screen or a doorway where the actors can slip out of sight for a second. At the right moment in the story, as the two characters lay down to sleep, the children should be briefed to secretly switch cloaks behind the screen. The two return keeping their identities hidden by pulling the cloaks over their faces.

The Story:

In the first century after Jesus, Christians began to spread his message across the world. Some followers of Jesus brought the Christian faith to Britain. At the same time Roman invaders came to occupy this country bringing with them their own Roman gods to worship. Where ever they went they told the people that Caesar, their Emperor, was the one to be worshiped, and anyone caught speaking about this Jesus would be put to death. Nevertheless, the stories about Jesus, his death and resurrection, continued to spread, and there were those who were even willing to die rather than give up the name of Jesus.

One Roman soldier, whose name was Alban, came to Britain along with thousands of other soldiers. Alban was a good soldier who served his Emperor well, had risen to the rank of centurion and was in charge of a hundred men.

One night Alban was making his way across the hillside, alone. He wrapped his thick cloak about him and wished himself back in Italy where the climate was a lot kinder than this freezing island. As he journeyed he came upon a small hut on the hillside. Knocking at the door he hoped to find someone who might provide him with something to eat. He was in luck. The door was opened by a man wearing a coarse, brown cloak.

"Come in, come in, my friend," said the man beckoning to his guest to come inside. There, in front of Alban was a simple wooden table and a roaring fire in the grate. Above the fire hung a black pot which was bubbling and simmering away.

"Come and have some warm soup and bread," said the owner of the house.

Alban took off his helmet and sat down, taken aback by the man's cheery welcome. Surely, thought Alban, this man can see that I am a Roman Soldier, and that I might do him some harm. But he was cold and the soup was warm, and so he sat down and the two began to talk.

Alban explained that he was on patrol and that the soldiers would be here in the morning to seek out Christians who had refused to worship the Emperor, Caesar. The man then told Alban that he was a monk, a follower of Jesus. He began to tell Alban stories from the Bible, about how Jesus had been put to death on a Roman Cross and how his followers had said that he was alive again. Alban listened. He had never heard anything like this before. Late into the night they talked and Alban made as if to leave but the owner insisted that Alban stay and sleep by his warm fire.

As Alban lay down he thought over everything the monk had said. He realised that soldiers would come in the morning and that the monk's life would be in danger. As the two men wrapped their cloaks around them Alban decided on a plan.

Early the next morning a red cloaked figure of a Roman soldier slipped out into the early morning mist. Later, a patrol of soldiers came knocking at the hut.

"We have come seeking those who call themselves Christians. We know that this is the dwelling of a monk, one who follows Jesus. Come out and give yourself up."

A man, his cloak pulled tightly over his head, appeared at the door.

"This must be the man," said one of the soldiers. "Take him away!"

They had not gone very far on the journey back to the Roman fort where they would try the man, when the man's cloak slipped from his face. It was Alban. In the time taken to travel this short distance the monk, on Alban's instruction, had escaped to safety.

Alban told the governor of that province that he had become a Christian. Refusing to give up the name of Jesus, days later, Alban was executed for his beliefs. He became the first Christian martyr (someone who has died for what they believe).

Today, if you go to a place called St Albans, in Hertfordshire, you can see the remains of a Roman wall against which Alban may have sheltered; beyond this stands a great Abbey named in Alban's honour.

Prayer:

Dear God,

We thank you for the Story of Alban who was willing to give his life for a friend. In smaller ways than this may we learn to be generous to our friends and those around us each day.
Amen.

Follow Up:

Write an imaginary letter of thanks as if you are the monk in the story. How would you feel about what had happened? Would you be more, or less, likely to continue to tell others about your beliefs after this? It is a fact that more people in the world today face religious persecution and suffer, and even die, for what they believe, than at any other time in history. Find out about organisations which campaign and support such people.

The Lighthouse Girl

The True Story of Grace Darling

Theme: Helping others.

Preparation:
Bring in a torch. Ask the children whether they can see the light beam it casts. Would you see it better in a dark room? How useful would it be if you were lost in a forest at night...or lost at sea?

The Story:

What do you think it would be like to live in a lighthouse? It might be exciting to be at the seaside everyday, or have rooms that are perfectly round and windows that all look out over the sea. In the good weather you might watch all kinds of ships sailing by. In the winter, when the wind whips the sea into crashing walls of water, it might be frightening. On such days as this you would want to stay inside where it feels safe. On days like this you would not want to get in to a little boat and go rowing. But that's just what the girl in this true story did.

Grace lived on the Longstone lighthouse on Brownsman Island, just off the coast of Northumberland. The task of looking after the lighthouse was an important one; many ships sailed that stretch of the North Sea and needed to be warned of the dangerous rocks that surrounded the coastline. Grace watched her father everyday as he went about his duties. The lamp had to be checked and the glass polished so that its light would be seen clearly by passing sailors. Grace enjoyed the visits by the men who delivered their supplies of food and other essentials every few weeks, for she had no company on the lonely rock which was her home for much of the year. What she enjoyed best of all, on a calm summer's day, was to go fishing with her father. Grace learned to row a small, flat bottomed boat called a coble, when she was still only young, and the two of them would enjoy seeing who would be the first to catch a mackerel for tea.

Grace never dreamed that her skills as an oarswoman would be needed to save lives.

On September 6th, in the year 1838, Grace went to her room and snuggled down under her blankets. Outside the wind howled and the waves crashed over the rocks at the side of the lighthouse. Every so often a large wave lifted and sent its spray spattering against the window where Grace tried to sleep. There had been no fishing trip today.

"It's far too rough for our little boat," said her father, "bigger boats than ours might be afraid of such a storm." And with that he went again to check on the lamp that shone out across the angry waters, warning ships of the dangerous rocks on this coastline.

Grace awoke early the next morning. She climbed into her coat and stepped out into the cold autumn air. The wind still whistled against the white walls of the lighthouse, and the waves tossed angrily against the black rocks out to sea. There in the distance, Grace could see the mast of a tall ship. It was rocking violently from side to side in the wind. Even at this distance, perhaps nearly a mile off, Grace could see that the ship was in trouble. She raced back into the lighthouse and scrambled up the stairs. Panting for breath Grace reached the top and swung the big telescope towards the bobbing masts of the ship. Already she could tell that it was very serious. The ship was listing half in, half out of the water and large pieces of wreckage were being tossed onto the black rocks nearby. And there, on the rocks, Grace was sure that something was moving. Straining hard into the lens of the old telescope she made out the shapes of several people clinging to the rocks.

"Father!" she shouted and ran to find him.

"What is it?" he asked, seeing that something terrible had happened from the expression on his daughter's face.

Grace quickly explained what she had seen and the two of them put on their waterproof coats and lifted the old coble down from its rack.

Mr Darling looked at his daughter. She was no longer a little girl, she was a young woman of twenty three, but this would put them both in great danger.

Grace, knowing what he was thinking, said, "You can't go alone. Two of us will row faster than one. The survivors may have little time left."

Her father knew she was right and in no time they were rowing hard against the fierce wind that threatened to capsize the little boat. Every wave seemed determined to keep them from their task but they would not give way. They both knew that the lives of the people on the stricken vessel were in their hands.

After what seemed an age, the fierce tide taking them ever away from their destination, they at last reached the wreck. Large bits of wood, a piece of rope and other fragments from the ship were thrown against the rocks where several people clung on for their lives. Grace counted about nine people, both men and women.

"Hold the boat steady while I pull them aboard," shouted her father against the howl of the wind and the crashing of waves against rock.

Grace's arms aching from the strain, pulled hard on the oars to steady the small craft. Each time the boat threatened to break against the jagged shapes that loomed out of the water, but Grace used all of her skill and every ounce of her strength to steady the boat. Then, one at a time, five of the survivors stumbled, wet and bedraggled, into the small rowing boat. Battling again against the strong current and the strong winds Grace and her father rowed back to the lighthouse. Two of the survivors from the wreck, experienced sailors, agreed to return for the others with Grace's father. Grace agreed to remain and take care of those who lay shivering, but glad to be alive. She had soon found warm blankets for them and she set a pan of hot soup to bubble on the stove.

The story of how Grace had rescued the survivors of "The Forfarshire" disaster soon spread and Grace's picture appeared in magazines and newspapers across the country.

Some say that Grace was never very strong after her exhausting struggle on that stormy morning in September. She died some years later and a monument was set up in her honour in the churchyard at Bamburgh, which can be seen by ships passing that coastline: 'To Grace Darling, the first Lifeboat Hero.'

Prayer:

Dear God,

Let us think of all those people who have helped us: our parents, our family, teachers and other adults at school, our friends. May we make up our minds to be helpful to others today.
Amen.

Follow Up:

Make a list of all the ways you can think of to help other people you know. Find out about the National Lifeboat Institution and other organisations which help people. Could you raise money for a good cause by holding a sponsored event or by selling home made biscuits and cakes?

Taming the Wolf

The Legend of St Francis of Assisi

Theme: Helping Others.

Preparation: *None.*

The Story:

"I've seen it, again. The wolf!" cried the old lady.

"Where?" asked her terrified neighbour.

"It came right down the street and stopped at my gate."

"What did you do?"

"Do? There's nothing you can do! I just ran inside my house and shut the door."

The Italian people of Gubbio were scared for their lives. For weeks they were afraid of leaving their houses because of the wolf that came regularly into town. At night they locked and bolted their doors and hid under covers and blankets. In the day they only went a short way to the end of their gardens or fields, and then only to count their chickens, or put their cattle safely into barns. No one dared venture far into the fields; crops went untended and withered in the hot sun. The only conversation, as people huddled in shop doorways, was where the wolf would strike next. The townspeople were even afraid to let their children play out in the street for fear that the wolf may come and carry one of them away.

Every now and then a band of men, armed with clubs, swords and pitchforks, would be persuaded to seek out and kill the wolf. But, each time, they had not gone far when their nerves failed them and they would return home with stories of how the wolf had attacked them, and how they were forced to flee for their lives.

Not far away there lived a man whose name was Francis. Francis was a monk. He had given his life to following Jesus Christ, and he lived among a community of monks who lived a simple life tending their vegetable gardens, praying and singing hymns to God. Francis had a love of animals. When it was his turn to work in the monastery garden he would often stop and whistle gently to the birds that came and watched him from the trees. Often they would fly down and settle on his coarse woollen robe, and sing to him as he worked. Rabbits, squirrels and other creatures would scamper out of the undergrowth just to be near to the one everyone knew as Brother Francis.

One day Francis got to hear about the wolf who was terrorising the people of Gubbio. He decided that he would go himself to meet the wolf. He arrived in the town with his coarse woollen robe tied at the waist with a simple rope, and a pair of sandals on his feet. At first the people laughed at him.

"How do you think that you can succeed on your own when others have failed?" they asked.

"But I shall not be alone. I have my companion, Brother Bernard here. And besides, God will accompany me on my journey too."

The men offered him their weapons, fierce looking clubs, swords and sharp pitchforks but Francis politely smiled and waved them away. He set off with his companion toward the forest where the wolf was said to have his lair. When they had gone a little way under the dark canopy of the trees, they heard a blood-curdling howl.

Bernard, standing near to Francis, gripped his friend's cloak tightly and begged him to return, but Francis continued onward.

Then, climbing up a short, rocky slope, they saw him. The great wolf looked down at the two men from the entrance to a dark cave.

Behind the wolf lay the carcass of a sheep that the wolf had taken earlier from a nearby field. The wolf stepped forward and bared its yellow teeth. It gave a low growl. Poor Bernard stepped back several paces, but Francis did not move. The wolf crouched low and began to come slowly toward Francis. It was puzzled that the man did not run away like all the others of his kind had done before him.

Then Francis spoke to the wolf. "Brother Wolf you have disobeyed our Master by attacking his creatures. In the name of The Lord Jesus I command you not to hurt anyone ever again."

And with that, to the astonishment of Bernard watching from the safety of a tree, the wolf walked slowly up to Francis . . . and licked his hand. Imagine the surprise of the townspeople when Francis arrived back in Gubbio with the wolf trotting obediently by his side. At first they ran inside and slammed shut their doors and windows, but, seeing that Francis was unharmed, they appeared from their houses to see the miracle that had taken place. After that the wolf no longer troubled them; and Francis saw to it that the wolf was fed scraps from each family's table so that the townspeople and the wolf lived at peace with each other for the rest of their days.

Prayer:

Dear God,

Help us to be kind to animals and thoughtful about all living creatures.
Amen.

Follow Up:

Talk about people who are cruel to animals. Hold a debate on an issue about animal rights, for example, fox-hunting (someone may have to agree to argue a point they are not in favour of to balance the debate). Or perhaps you can do something practical, like making bird feeders. Hang them out and watch the birds come and feast.

Playground
Rules O.K.

STORIES SET IN SCHOOL ABOUT
HOW WE TREAT OTHERS

Playground Rules O.K.

Who Cares?

Losers Weepers

Sweets

Mr Whittle

Playground Rules O.K.

Theme: Why we need rules.

Preparation:
Bring in a poster of road signs. Ask the children why rules are needed on the road. Tell them today's story is about someone who could not see the need for rules at all.

The Story:

"Why do we have to have rules all the time? They're just to stop you having fun, just things the teachers don't want you to do."

Bezza was complaining as usual. Her mates had heard it all before. The teachers just wanted to stop her having fun in school, doing the things she liked, wearing the clothes she liked, doing what she wanted when she wanted.

"You've got to have some rules," Katie began. "You can't just do what you want. Even grown ups have rules."

"No they don't," argued Bezza, "they don't have to go to bed at some stupid time, just when you want to watch your favourite programme, or finish your computer game."

Bezza loved computer games. Her Mum had just bought the latest one for her birthday. It was all about a magic castle and you had to find your way down the tunnels, solve the puzzles or complete the challenges to get to the next level. Bezza was already on level 17 and there were only three to go before she would be supreme champion. Anyone who reached the magical level twenty could send away for a new game, free from the makers. To get the prize you had to find the special password that was hidden somewhere in level twenty. As soon as school was finished Bezza would go home and play for an hour before tea, and then she would watch her favourite programme, and then she might hope to sneak in for another session after that. Bezza's Mum did not let her go on the computer for more than an hour each day. It was another rule and Bezza as usual complained bitterly about it.

"It's not fair! All my friends are allowed." (Bezza's Mum knew this meant one other person.). "They don't have to stop at six-o-clock. It's my computer and I ought to be allowed to go on when I want. It's a stupid rule and I don't see why I should have to stop just when I'm nearly going to win."

40

"Well that's the rule, and you're just going to have to put up with it," said Bezza's Mum. "It may be your computer, young lady, but it's my hard earned money that paid for it, so I can set the rules in this house."

"Rules, rules, rules!" muttered Bezza, under her breath. "They're just there to stop you having fun."

At school the next day Bezza was coming out of assembly. She was desperate to see her friends. She pushed past the smaller children who were in her way and ran down the long corridor. Smack! She ran right into Mrs Corbishley, the Deputy Head.

"Just what do you think you're doing, Bethany Hughes?"

When someone used your proper name it was always bad news.

"Sorry Miss, I was just in a hurry to get out."

"Well, you know the rules. No running in the corridor. Now you can go and sit in my room during playtime and write out the school rules. There's a copy on my desk."

Bezza sighed and shuffled down the corridor towards Mrs Corbishley's room.

"A good job I wasn't carrying a cup of hot coffee!" muttered the teacher.

This last remark was lost on Bezza. Writing out the rules, that was just the worst thing she could have made her do. What was the point of rules anyway?

That night Bezza turned on her game. She forgot all about school and those stupid rules. Here she was master in her own land, a land filled with giants and dragons and goblins. A world full of castles, turrets, dungeons and long, dark tunnels.

"You have entered level 17," said the computer voice. "Proceed with caution. The Castle Master awaits you. Follow his instructions."

While the next level was loading up Bezza turned away to pick up her chocolate bar. She did not see the message which quickly flashed behind her: "GAME MALFUNCTION. CANCEL EXISTING PROGRAMME. INSTRUCTION. TURN OFF YOUR COMPUTER."

As Bezza turned back the green lettering disappeared and the walls of the castle again filled the picture.

"When is a castle door not a door?" asked the Castle Master.

"That's easy," thought Bezza and typed: WHEN IT IS AJAR

"CORRECT. Return to level 17 and try again."

"That's not supposed to happen!" said Bezza aloud, "I should go on when I get a question right, not back. That's the rule."

"Climb through the window and find the magic key."

Using the mouse control Bezza climbed through the window and opened the trap-door in the dimly lit room.

"You have failed to find the key. The key is in The Dragon's Lair."

"That's not fair. You didn't say it was somewhere else. You showed me the princess' bedroom. That's not playing by the rules!"

Level 16 flashed on the screen. "If you collect thirteen apples from the garden you may return to the princess' bedroom for the key," said the expressionless voice.

"But you said the key was there before, and it wasn't. What's the point in going there?"

But Bezza had to try. Quickly moving her screen character along the maze of passageways and corridors she came into a fluorescent-green garden. There in the middle was an apple tree. Bezza counted the apples on it. There were twelve.

"But the rules are that you can't ask me to collect something if it isn't there. How can I know what I'm supposed to do if you don't play by the rules?" Bezza shouted at the screen.

"Return to level 15."

Bezza had had enough. She turned the screen off.

The next day on the playground Mrs Corbishley politely asked a group of girls not to stand behind the shed. Seeing Bezza she expected the usual string of complaints.

"Sorry Miss," said Bezza. "I forgot the rule. We shouldn't be where a teacher can't see us. It's for our safety." There was not a hint of sarcasm in her voice, either.

4 2

The teacher nearly dropped her coffee in surprise!

Prayer:

Dear God,

Help us to realise that rules are there to help us.
Help us to try to keep rules for our good and the good of others.
Amen.

Follow Up:

Think of a rule in school. Talk about all the possible consequences for other people of breaking the rule. Is it O.K. for some to follow the rules and not others? Imagine a world where everyone broke the rules all the time. Would it be a nice place to live? Invent your own class rules.

Who Cares?

Theme: Giving our best.

Preparation:
Borrow a school bag from one of the children in school. Put in a pencil case, a lunch box, some P.E. kit, perhaps even some football boots if available. Ask children to put their hands up if they pack their own school bag each night. Does Mum or someone at home do it for you? Meanwhile pack the items into the bag as you say that today's story is about someone who was not very good at looking after his own school bag. A football boot taken from the bag at the right moment in the story adds a touch of drama to the telling!

The Story:

Jaz turned up late for school as usual.

"I hadn't got my lunch!" was the explanation he offered to Mr Sykes, his long suffering teacher.

"Well hurry up and sit down and stop smirking at everyone will you." Jaz Williams was often late or he had no pencil for the lesson or he had left his homework at home. It was always the same story.

"Lend us a pencil, will you," whispered Jaz to his friend Rob.

"Why haven't you got one? I'm always lending you a pencil…and I never get it back."

"Turn to page 15, everyone and do the first ten sums, please."
Jaz put his hand up.

"I haven't got a book."

"Everyone else took a book home for homework and they brought it back," said an irritated Mr Sykes.

"Well, my Mum forgot to put it in my bag, didn't she."
The teacher sighed. It was much the same as usual. It was never Jaz's fault.

"Have you done the homework?"

"No, I didn't remember to take my homework book home. I took the maths book but I didn't know what questions to do."

Mr Sykes sighed again and, turning his attention away from Jaz began the lesson.

"Who cares about stupid homework anyway?" whispered Jaz to his friend, who was trying to start his work. "If you're going to play football for England you're not going to do sums while you're playing are you?"
Rob had heard this one before...many times!

It was true that Jaz was a good footballer. He was captain of the school team. Mr Sykes was the football teacher. He had put Jaz forward for trials and he had been chosen to play for the county side. Rob played for the school too, but he was not good enough to play for the county.

This afternoon there was to be a very important match played here at school, the semi-final of the Primary School's Cup. Everyone would be there to watch. One more game and then the final, and the possibility of actually winning the cup. It was what they had all dreamed of for the last three weeks.

The afternoon could not go quickly enough. It was Technology in the afternoon and they were making puppets. Jaz and Rob were going to make theirs into two England footballers.

"Will you lend me some of that white material?" Jaz asked Rob. "I didn't bring any in. My Mum didn't have any."

Rob cut off a piece. He knew Jaz was lying. He had just not bothered to think about it the night before.

Mr Sykes came over. "I see you are relying on your friend again, Jaz. You really must learn to get organised yourself. You'll never manage at secondary school you know."

"Who cares!" said Jaz, when the teacher had gone. "I'll worry about that when I get there won't I?"

Then, at last, it was the end of the day . . . . and time for the match.

Rob pulled out the kitbag from the cupboard and started giving out the shirts. It was really the captain's job but it was hopeless expecting Jaz to do anything like that.

Suddenly there was a shout. It was Jaz.
"ONE BOOT!" cried Jaz. "Look, my Mum's gone and only put in one football boot."

"Are you sure?" said Rob. "Here, let me have a look."

But it was true.

"Why didn't you pack your bag yourself?" said Shareen, the team's striker. Jaz did not bother to answer.

Mr Sykes came over, and without much sympathy he sent Jaz off to look in lost property for a spare pair. No luck! They tried the cloakroom and managed to turn up a muddy pair of trainers, but they were the wrong size. Jaz frantically ran down to the office to make a phone call, but he knew that his Mum would not be there. He was right.

"There's nothing else for it. Samantha will have to play instead," said Mr Sykes, running a hand across his forehead.

Rob looked at his friend who had nothing left to say. The team trooped out onto the pitch and Jaz, still in his school uniform ambled on to the touchline to watch. Although Shareen scored a brilliant goal the team went on to lose the match. There would be no cup-final this year. At the end of the day the team packed their bags and went home . . . but one player went home and, for the first time, packed his own bag!

Prayer:

Dear God,

Thank you for all the things we use each day at school. Thank you for pens and pencils, paints and crayons, our sports kit and playground games. May we take care of what we have and learn, with each new day, to become responsible for ourselves.
Amen.

Follow up:

Play 'I packed my school bag and I put in . . . . . .' Each person has to repeat the last item and add one item alphabetically, so 'I put in an apple, a banana, a crayon' etc. Talk about responsibilities. What other responsibilities do you have at home or at school? Is it fair to have to be responsible for ourselves and our belongings?

Losers Weepers

Theme: Honesty/Thinking of others.

Preparation:
Have a ten pound note secreted in your hand which can be 'found' on the floor at the right moment in the story. Losers Weepers may be easily adapted as a story for Mother's Day or other special occasions.

The Story:

The whistle had gone and Billy was about to line up when something caught his eye. He bent down and there was a ten pound note on the playground. He looked about but no one was paying him any attention. Billy picked up the note and slipped it into his pocket. It was going to be a good day today, he could tell.

The classes lined up and filed into the red brick building. Once inside Mrs Bryan called the register and everyone was there except Emma Newell. Typical! Billy's class were going to get the prize this week for 100% attendance; at least they would have if only Emma was here today. It was just like a girl to be selfish, thought Billy, staying away just to stop everyone else winning the prize.

Just then Emma Newell came in. She looked as if she had been crying. Typical, thought Billy again. She's probably fallen out with her Mum before school, or she's forgotten to do her homework again. Then it was Maths and everyone got out their books and Mrs Bryan showed them the sums they had to do on page 24. The lesson dragged on and Billy chewed the end of his pencil. He began to think of the things he might buy with his ten pound note. He could buy a whole week's supply of chocolate bars; he could put the money towards a new C.D. by that new group on the television last night. He could put it in his money box and save up enough to buy the new football boots he badly wanted now he had been picked to play for the school team.

"Put your things away children. It's playtime," said the teacher.

Outside on the playground Billy played 'it' with his friends. Ryan got him and then it was Billy's turn to chase. He stood and counted to ten. "One pound, two pound, three pound," he counted out loud. It was then that he saw Emma Newell again. She was still crying and now she was wandering round the playground on her own. Billy knew that he ought to ask her what the matter was. But she was a girl and he wasn't going to look daft in front of his mates. One of the girls could ask her instead. It was what girls were good at and boys weren't. Everyone knew that. Billy got to ten and charged off after the boys who had now scattered to all parts of the playground.

The day seemed to last for ever but, eventually, it was home time. Billy grabbed his bag and dashed out of the door nearly knocking Emma Newell over in the corridor as he went. He ran all the way to the shop. When he got there he pressed his nose to the glass and surveyed the wonders inside the shop. There were boxes of penny chews, liquorice bootlaces, fizzy cola bottles, sweets in packets; Mr Patel even had the old fashioned jars of sweets that you could have weighed on the old scales and poured into a paper bag.

As he cast his eyes over the treats he let his fingers crumple the note in his pocket just to check it was real. It was! Finders Keepers! Losers Weepers! That's what everyone said. If you were careless enough to lose your dinner money on the playground then it was your fault. Then Billy saw it. The Sticker Album in glossy and sparkly colour at the front of the shop window. It had all the latest Premiership Footballers and there was a starter set of 50 stickers free with the album. Billy looked at the price. It was £9.99. Just right!

In no time at all Billy was coming out of the shop with his album clutched under his arm. But, just as he turned the corner of the road, he stopped. There was Emma Newell and her friend Charlotte sitting on a bench. Billy stopped in his tracks. For some reason he did not want them to see him. He could hear what they were saying from where he stood.

" . . . and its my Mum's birthday and she's in hospital and I had a ten pound note that my Gran gave me and I was going to get my Mum some flowers and now I've lost it I won't be able to buy her anything."

Billy looked down at his new album. He looked back at the two girls at the bench and then he hurried home. Before dinner Billy got his album out and looked through the pages. The glossy colours beckoned to him from inside the cellophane packaging. Somehow he could not bring himself to open it. He kept thinking about Emma and her Mum in hospital. He looked at the clock and, knowing that Mr Patel's shop would stay open for another half an hour Billy decided what he must do.

At school next day Billy found a home-made card in his desk. He did not let anyone else see it because it was from a girl. Inside it simply said . . . THANK YOU.

Billy smiled.

Prayer:

Dear God,

Help us to use our imagination to think how others may feel. Help us to treat other people as we would like to be treated ourselves. Amen.

Follow up:

Put two people in the middle of the circle as Emma and Billy. Interview them and ask them why they behaved as they did at each point in the story. How did they feel? Imagine different scenarios (what if Billy had kept the album?) What makes us choose to do 'the right thing?'

Sweets

Theme: Racism.

Preparation:
A packet of coloured sweets will add to the telling of this story. If you think you can get away with it you might give out one or two sweets to a few children before you begin (selections must be random, for example, to blonde haired children and without explanation, not for valid reasons such as sitting up nicely!). This will create an atmosphere of curiosity before you begin.

The Story:

"That's a good answer, Charandeep. Well done."

The teacher leaned forward and offered a red shiny sweet in his hand. Charandeep leaned forward to accept but Miss Gover swept the prize past her outstretched hand and gave it instead to the girl behind.

"What lovely green eyes you have, Melinda," said the teacher, as she returned to the front of the class. She then shook the tube and gave another sweet to a brown haired boy sitting in the front row, who had said nothing all lesson.

"Who can tell me what 10 times 24 is?"

Another hand went up, but not Charandeep's. She sat slumped in her chair her head bowed forward. She was not going to get caught again.

James Corrigan answered this time. "240, Miss."

"That's correct, James."

No sweet.

"20 times 24, then? Anyone."

You could almost hear the brains ticking.

"440, Miss."

"No, that's not right, Bryony. Good try, though."

"It's 480, Miss."

"Yes, it is Sarah. You forgot to double the tens column, Bryony," said Miss Gover, and as she did so she walked across and gave a sweet to the mousy haired girl who had got the sum wrong. Returning to the white board the teacher had to go by Sarah's desk.

"480, Miss," Sarah repeated, but Miss Gover ignored her. Instead she walked back to the front, shook the packet, and gave two sweets to Emily who sat still and quiet near the teacher's desk.

At playtime the children got together.

"It's just not fair. What's she playing at?"

"I don't know do I!"

"What's the point of all this sweet stuff. . . if you're not going to get one if you get a question right?"

Charandeep listened to the arguments but she said nothing.

"Well I reckon it's up to Miss what she does. It's her classroom. She can give sweets to who she likes."

"Well that's easy for you to say. You got one and we didn't."

"Well perhaps I got it for being good, or something," said Bryony Jones.

"What's good about not answering the questions?"

"You're just jealous that Miss likes us more than you," said Sarah Manning, and the two girls put their noses in the air and walked off to another part of the playground.

It was the same in Literacy and, after a while some of the children gave up answering questions at all. The same people got more sweets. By the time dinnertime came they were really cross.

"Just what's going on?" said Matthew.

"I think she's flipped," replied Ahmed, rolling his eyes to show that he thought Miss was going mad.

Charandeep looked at the faces of the children standing in the group by the P.E. shed. They were all the ones who had not been given a sweet. It was no big deal. No one expected a sweet for getting the answer right. It was just the unfairness of it all.

As she looked across the playground there, by the climbing frame, was another group of children. They looked back towards Charandeep and laughed. She studied each face in turn. They were all the ones who had been given sweets all morning. Did Miss Gover not realise the harm she was doing? Already there were friends who were not speaking to each other over this stupid game.

In the afternoon it was R.E. Everyone settled down as the teacher put a video into the player.

She was too busy thinking about the morning to take notice straight away of the programme they were supposed to be watching. But, after a while the voice captured her attention. The old black and white pictures told the story of how black Americans had been treated badly years ago in America. A man in a dark suit was standing and talking to a huge crowd:

"I have a dream that one day my four little children will be judged not by the colour of their skin but by the content of their character."

When the programme finished the teacher showed them some more pictures in a book and explained that white men in America in the 1920s made people travel on different buses, they were not allowed to vote, apply for good jobs or go to university simply because their skin was a different colour.

"How do you think they felt?" asked Miss Gover.

No one answered at first. Then Charandeep put her hand up.

"Miss, they must have felt like some of us did this morning when you treated us differently. Is that why you did it?"

"Go on," smiled the teacher.

"And it must have been much worse than that, because they would have been treated badly every day, all the time, because they were black."

"That's right, Charandeep. You are very clever to have worked it out. I gave sweets only to those children who have blue or green eyes. I am sorry that I may have made some of you feel bad for a while but I wanted you to understand just a little bit about what it was like for these people to be treated differently just because of their skin colour." And with that Miss Gover went to all the children who had been given nothing that day and made up for what they had missed.

Reflection:

Let us think for a moment about the way we treat other people. Are we fair in the way we behave towards other people? Are we unkind to others simply because they look different to us in some way? Let us all try to change our world for the better by treating others with respect.

Follow Up:

Think about how easily we pick on the differences of others when we want to hurt someone. Older children may reflect on the life of someone who was a victim of, or campaigned against, racial hatred, like, Anne Frank, Nelson Mandela, Martin Luther King etc.

Mr Whittle

Theme: Treating older people with respect.

Preparation:

As children arrive for assembly begin sharpening (whittling) a piece of wood with a craft knife from the technology trolley. You can break off from this activity to tell the story. Alternatively a ship in a bottle, which features in the story, is an interesting item to show if you can get hold of one. You might ask the children how they think the ship got in there. Save explanations until the end to keep up the suspense.

The Story:

Darren was on his way home when he saw him. The old man was in his shed doorway again. The garden was a real untidy state. Grass higher than your ankles and the flower beds were overgrown with a tangle of weeds and bits of plant that had long since died. There he was wearing that stupid hat with the metal badge on it, messing about in that old wooden shed like he was doing something useful.

Darren lived next door to Mr Whittle and Darren's Mum sometimes complained, to no one in particular, about the overgrown garden. She wished that he would keep it a bit better. All the weeds grew into their garden and it just spoiled the whole look of the neighbourhood, she said.

"Stupid old man!" muttered Darren to his mates as they crossed over the road, "why doesn't he go and live somewhere else? His garden's a mess, his house is a mess and he's a mess. He's just in the way."

Without thinking Darren picked up a stone and threw it. There was the sound of breaking glass. The stone had gone straight through Mr Whittle's kitchen window. The old man's head appeared out of the shed and Darren and his mates ducked down.

"What 'you do that for?" hissed Gary from under the fence post where they hid.

"I dun'no. I just felt like it. Silly old fool. He didn't even know it was us."

"It wasn't us," continued Gary. "It was you. I'm not getting the blame if he comes round our school to get you into trouble with Mrs Wallasey. Anyway you could have hurt the old bloke. What's he ever done to you?"

"I just think he's stupid, that's all. And he won't come around 'cause he's too slow to see what's going on anyway."

The next day at school there was Mr Whittle. He was standing at the doorway to Darren's classroom. Worse still he was talking to Darren's teacher, Mr Pipe.

The class were in the middle of a technology lesson. They were making buggies out of wood and there were hacksaws and hammers and drills everywhere.

"Stop, everyone," said the teacher. "This is Mr Whittle. He lives nearby to our school and he's come to help us this afternoon."

The class settled back down to work. Darren breathed a sigh of relief. The old man had not come to complain about someone who had thrown a stone through his window. Then Mr Whittle came right over to where Darren was working.

"Do you need any help?" smiled the old man.

"Er, yes please!" muttered Darren, not wanting to be rude to the newcomer, not with Mr Pipe in earshot.

Over the next few minutes Mr Whittle expertly showed Darren how to cut a piece of wood straight, how to make a right angled corner and how to drill through a wheel to fit an axle. His old hands seemed like sandpaper to Darren but he watched fascinated as Mr Whittle nimbly worked the wood as if it were a part of his own hand. When they had finished the old man slipped something out of his coat pocket.

"Do ya' see this?" he asked, holding up the tiny hull of a sailing ship carved out of wood. On the deck of the ship were three tiny masts laying down. He took a craft knife form the tray and expertly took a few slices off the bow of the ship until it was a perfectly smooth shape. "I'm going to put this in a bottle back home tonight. Do you want to see?"

Darren wanted to but he was afraid to ask.

"It's alright you can ask your Mum first, check it's O.K. Your Mum can see us from the window. I only live next door."

That evening, in the light from the shed, Darren watched amazed as Mr Whittle tied a piece of cotton to the tiny masts and eased the ship into the bottle. Slowly but gently he pulled on the cotton until the masts stood up on the deck. Then he released the thread and put a cork into the opening of the bottle and there was a beautiful ship riding on the sea all contained in a little glass bottle.

"Mr Whittle?" began Darren, trying to find the words, "I've got something to tell you."

"You've no need, lad," said the old man. "I know it was you who broke my window."

"But why did you not say anything?"

"I figured that if I had told your teacher then we might not be friends. Perhaps we can repair that window together at the weekend. My fingers are O.K. but I can't lift my arms so well now I'm older. But you could do a good job I'm sure."

Darren looked up at Mr Whittle and smiled.

Prayer:

Dear God,

Sometimes we do not understand older people. They do not dress as we do, behave in the same way or like the things that we like. May we remember that the older generation has made the world we enjoy today. They have often lived through hard times and made sacrifices for us. May we learn from their experience and benefit from their wisdom.
Amen.

Note:
This may be a suitable moment to remind children about safety issues, not going with strangers etc. (In the story Darren's Mum knows exactly where her son is and can see him all the time from her kitchen window).

Follow Up:
Share good experiences of old people (take care as there may be someone who has lost a grandparent recently). Think why they say the things they do. Think about ways that you might benefit from talking to older people (safely). Think about things you might do for older people in the community.

The Shepherd Boy

A SERIES ON THE LIFE OF DAVID

The Shepherd Boy
Don't Judge a Book by its Cover
Defeating Giants
Friends and Enemies
One Bad Turn Deserves . . .

The Shepherd Boy

David looks after his sheep

Theme: Courage.

Preparation:
Begin by explaining that you will be telling a story in several parts. Children will be very familiar with this concept as many of them will be avid watchers of television soaps. If using this material over several weeks you may want to ask the children to help you to recap the story so far, each time.

The Story:

David was a shepherd boy.

He worked out on the hillside of Palestine looking after the sheep for his father. David was the youngest in the family; his older brothers were mostly away from home fighting in the king's army. Sometimes David wondered what it would be like to be a soldier, to wear bright armour and carry a great sword. But David did not mind being a shepherd boy.

There was enough to do looking after sheep. You had to make sure that they were led out to find some lush green grass to eat and be able to drink from a clean, fresh stream of cool water. At night-time you had to count the sheep and see that every single one was safely shut in the fold. And then there were the wild animals.

On the hillsides where David lived there were lions and bears who were always on the lookout for a tasty sheep to steal and take back to their den. It was David's job to see that they did not succeed.

One day, when David was sitting watching the sheep grazing by the water's edge, a shadow appeared over his shoulder. There was his older brother, Eliab. Like all older brothers Eliab enjoyed making fun of the youngest.

"I see you are very busy, little David," he laughed. "Never mind! Someday you will be able to do a man's job, and be a soldier like me."

"Perhaps I will," replied David. "But until then I have a job to do here, and I am going to do the best I can to keep my father's valuable flock safe."

"Just go back to your sheep, David," said Eliab, with a sneer, "and mind you don't strain yourself lying down in the sun."

David knew that it was not worth a reply, and he waved as Eliab strode off, his great sword clanking against his thick legs as he walked.

David lay back against the tree that shaded him from the hot midday sun. The sheep were munching lazily on the grass that grew by the side of the refreshing mountain stream. David drew from his little bag a small harp, called a lyre. When he had time to sit and play David liked to write songs. (Many of the songs that David wrote can be read in the book of the Bible called The Psalms).

As David watched the sheep grazing by the stream the words of another song began to form in his mind. He thought about his work as a shepherd and he thought too of the God he had been brought up to follow. He began to think how much God was like a shepherd too, caring for his people like a shepherd looks after the sheep.

The Lord is my Shepherd.
I have everything I need
He lets me rest in fields of green grass
He leads me to quiet pools of fresh water . . . .

David plucked the strings of his lyre skillfully and began to compose a melody for the words that had formed in his mind. The rustling of the wind in the trees and the gentle chatter of the trickling water seemed to join in the music . . . but there was another sound. David stopped playing. There it was again.

David knew the sounds of the hillside well. Perhaps he had been mistaken, though. Maybe it was just the wind in the trees. But no, there it was again, a sound he recognised, a sound that made the hairs on the back of his neck prickle. There was something in the bushes just beyond the grey rocks. Something coming this way. Something big. He listened again. There it was, unmistakably this time, the soft padding of large paws, the snuffle of a hungry bear.

David quickly looked about him. The sheep were unaware of the danger. They continued munching lazily on the grass. David knew that the bear could appear any moment. The young shepherd boy stood up quietly, as he did so he reached into his bag and drew out his sling. Tip-toeing to the waters edge David found two or three smooth, round stones and wiped them dry on his tunic. He checked to see if any sheep had wandered away from the water's edge. None of them had moved. David now crept across to the cover of an olive tree where he placed himself between the sheep and the place where the sound was coming from. Then he waited.

The pad, pad, pad, of the creature's great paws came again, and the sniffing, snorting, snuffling as the creature tried to pick up the scent that had led him this far. The bushes began to rustle, then shudder, then began to shake…and then the bear was out in the open, a huge animal three times the size of the little shepherd boy behind the tree.

It sniffed the air again, and then looked in the direction of the sheep. They continued eating, unaware of the danger. The bear had cleverly kept the wind at its back so that the sheep would not catch his scent.

As David looked he saw that a tiny lamb had strayed away from its mother. The great bear began to lumber towards it. It was only metres away now. Then David swiftly stepped out from behind the tree, and called out.

"Leave my father's sheep alone."

And with that the bear rose up on his hind legs and, turning to face the boy, gave a great roar. David let fly the stone that seconds earlier had been whirling in his sling. The stone flew . . . and struck the bear with a thud on the side of its head. With a yelp of pain, it ran off back into bushes, and disappeared from view. David gave chase to see that it did not return.

Later that day, Eliab arrived back from the battle field. There had been no fighting that day, and he still had enough energy to tease his little brother.

"Here you are again little, shepherd boy. Have you had a busy day, lying here in the sunshine?"

And then he stopped. Because, there, imprinted on the grass by David's foot was the biggest paw print Eliab had ever seen. He knew enough about the hillside to know that it was newly made. And, sticking out of David's bag, was a handful of the animal's brown fur.

Eliab stopped teasing David from that day onwards; the day that the shepherd boy had chased away the hungry bear. As David made his way home that night he wrote the next lines of his song in his head:

Even if I go through the deepest darkness,
I will not be afraid, Lord
For you are with me
Your shepherd's rod and staff protect me.

Prayer:

Dear God,

We thank you for the story of David and how he relied on you to help him when he was in danger. Help us to remember all those who are there to help us when we face difficulties, when we don't know what to do, or when we are afraid. Help us to be brave enough to ask for help when we need it.
Amen.

Follow Up:

Give everyone a piece of paper and a pencil. Ask everyone to write down the name or title of someone who helps us (dinner-supervisors, crossing-patrol etc.) On the back of the paper write down an occasion when you may be in need of help. Read out the situations and ask children to match situations to helpers. Discuss the answers. Talk about the need to ask for appropriate help in situations (for example, if you found a strange package on the playground would it be enough to tell your friends about it?)

Don't Judge a Book by its Cover

David is Chosen as King

Theme: How we judge other people.

Preparation:
Select two books, one a textbook with a striking cover design but on a subject of little interest to children, the second a great story for children but in a plain cover. Secondly, prepare small cards with the numbers 1 to 7 on them. Give these out to the tallest boys in the school just before the assembly. Number one should be the tallest, two the next, and so on. Instruct them to come out as you tell, or read, the story as each son is mentioned (e.g First he brought the oldest son . . .). Finally, as you mention David himself reach down and bring out the smallest boy you can see (often in the front row).

Introduction:
Begin by holding up your two books asking the children to choose which one they would like to read. You can "assist" their choice by describing the colour illustrations etc. on the first book but say little about the one with the plain cover.
Put the books down and say that you will tell the children more later on.

The Story:

A long time ago in Israel there was a man named Samuel who had a very important job. He was a listener. He had to listen to God and give His message to the people. It was not always easy.

At that time Israel had chosen their very first king. His name was Saul but he was not a very good king, and, very soon, Samuel found himself looking for a new king for Israel. This time he would have to get it right!

One morning he rose early, wrapped his cloak around him, and set off across the hillside towards the little hill town of Bethlehem. As he travelled he kept one eye on the hills around him for fear that any of Saul's men might see him. It would not do to let the king know just what he was about.

On the way he began to wonder to himself just what sort of a person God would choose. Would he be strong? Would he be tall or good looking? Would he be a great soldier? Samuel knew that a king might be all these things. But he also knew that God did not just look on the outside. A king would have to be good and wise and fair. These things were not always obvious from just looking at a person from the outside.

Soon he arrived at the house of a man named Jesse.

"This is where you will find your king," Samuel seemed to hear God whisper in his ear.

When Jesse opened the door to Samuel he stepped back in surprise.

"Good day, Samuel," said Jesse, "what brings you here?"

"I have come to choose a new king for your country Israel. God has told me that one of your sons will be the man whom God has chosen. Bring them before me then I may see who it is."

Jesse was amazed at these words but he went and did as he was told.

First he brought his oldest son, Eliab. Eliab was big and strong and already a soldier in the king's army. He would surely make a fine king.

Samuel looked at Eliab and God whispered in Samuel's ear.

"No he is not the one," said Samuel.

The next son was brought before Samuel. He too was a soldier and a champion with the sword. Is this the man Samuel wondered? Again the whisper.

"No he is not the one," said Samuel.

In came the next son. Although not as tall as the first two he was strong and athletic from working in his father's fields all day. But again Samuel said, "No he is not the one."

In turn another four sons were brought in, seven in all. Each one was carefully examined. But each was rejected.

"Are these all your sons Jesse?" asked Samuel.

"Well almost all," replied Jesse. "There is just one more but he is only a young shepherd boy. His name is David. But he is so very small and all he does all day is look after my sheep. I'm sure you would like to think again about one of my older sons."

"Bring him here," said Samuel.

In a few moments a small boy came in. He had black wiry hair and he looked a little puzzled at the crowd who had gathered in his father's house.

Samuel looked carefully at the small boy in front of him. He was not very tall. He did not have great broad shoulders like his brothers. It was unlikely that he could even lift a sword off the ground.

Samuel looked. God whispered in Samuel's ear.

"This is the one."

Conclusion:

You see with God's help Samuel could see something special in David. He knew that he would in time grow up to be good, kind and wise. He would make a good future king. We must also be careful of judging other people by what we see on the outside. It is what is on the inside that counts. Just like these two books that I showed you earlier. You see this one looks good on the outside but is (reveal the title/details etc.). Whereas this one does not look very promising on the outside but inside (reveal the title/details etc.).

Reflection:

Let us think about the people we look up to. Do we judge other people by what we see on the outside? Or do we value such qualities of goodness, kindness and fairness that make a person what they are on the inside. Think for a moment about how other people might see you.

Follow Up:

In the circle say who you admire and why. Are our choices based on external features, for example, athletic, good looking etc. What qualities do you value in your friends? How do we find out what people are really like?

Defeating Giants

The Story of David and Goliath

Theme: Trust.

Preparation:
Have three metre sticks to hand to show the height of Goliath. A gymnastic table or the caretaker's stepladder will serve to reach the full height required. Bring a small boy from the front row of the assembly hall to contrast with Goliath's size.

Introduction:
Begin saying that today's story tells of a battle between two people. One a giant (here you can indicate the height on the wall with metre sticks) and the other a young shepherd boy (bring a small boy forward for just a moment).

The Story:

The Israelites were at war with their great enemy, the Philistines. Day after day the two armies were ranged across the hillsides looking across at each other. Both had hundreds of soldiers at the ready in full battle armour, their swords and shields catching the midday sun as they waited for the command to go down into the valley to fight.

Suddenly, from between the ranks of the Philistine army stepped a great warrior. He was more like a tree than a man. The heads of the soldiers standing by him seemed barely to come up to his chest. In his hand he brandished a great sword as long as a man and his shield appeared so large that it seemed as if it would block out the sun itself.

"Who will come and fight against me?" roared the great giant, in a voice like crashing thunder. "We do not need to send our armies into battle. Come and send your best warrior to meet me in combat. If you beat me the Philistines will become your slaves, but if I win you shall serve us. Who is brave enough to face me down there in the valley?"

All of the Israelite soldiers looked at each other in fear. And no one was willing to go down and meet this monster of a man. Day after day Goliath came and shouted his taunts across at the Israelite army but there was no one who would go and stop his boasting.

It so happened one day that David was going to visit his eldest brother,

Eliab, at the battlefield, bringing him some bread and cheese for his lunch. He arrived just as Goliath was shouting again across the valley.

"Who will come and fight against me? Who is brave enough to face me down there in the valley?"

"Who is this man?" said David, not taking his eyes off the giant on the distant hillside.

"He is Goliath, the Philistine."

"But why are we letting him insult God's army like this?"

"What do you know?" sneered Eliab, "you are only a shepherd boy. What would you know about fighting?"

David looked up at his brother, anger flashing in his eyes. "Then if there is no one to go . . . I shall go!"

"What? Don't be so stupid. You are only a boy. How can you face this giant? Just go back to your sheep where you belong."

But David would not be silenced. He went on and on at his brother until, eventually, he found himself in the tent of King Saul.

"Who is this that you have brought before me?" asked the king.

"It is my young brother, David," said Eliab looking embarrassed. "He wants to fight Goliath.

All the men standing by laughed aloud.

"Well," said the king, "I admire your bravery but this is no task for a small boy. You should go home where it is safe."

But again David would not take no for an answer and he persuaded the king to let him go. King Saul beckoned to his attendants to bring some armour and a sword and shield. But when David put these things on they were so heavy he could hardly stand.

"I do not need these things," said David. "God will be on my side to help me."

A moment later David was striding down the hillside to meet the giant. When Goliath saw him coming he roared with laughter.

"What is this! Are you playing a joke on me? I shall eat this boy for breakfast."

"Goliath, I am coming to fight for my people, Israel, and for the honour of the name of my God. He will help me defeat you."

With a shout of rage Goliath began to walk down the hill to meet David. The ground seemed to shake with each footstep.

As David neared the middle of the valley he stopped and knelt down. There was a small stream trickling by and David reached in and took five small white stones. He then unfastened a sling from his belt, which he had used often to frighten away lions from his flock of sheep.

Standing up he put one stone into the sling. He began to wind up the strand of leather, faster, faster until it was just a blur in his hand. (This action can be mimed to heighten the drama.)

"Prepare to die, Israelite," shouted the giant . . . and then he clapped a hand to his forehead . . . and he fell down dead.

David, with God's help, had defeated the giant.

Prayer:

Dear God,

We thank you for the story of David and how he relied on you to defeat the giant that threatened his people. Help us to face up to the giants in our lives, those things which can make us afraid, playground bullies, the darkness, or fear of the unknown. Perhaps, then, as David did, we too may defeat our giants.
Amen.

Follow Up:

Talk about feelings. What makes us afraid? What can we do about our fears? Who can we talk to?

Friends and Enemies

The story of David and Jonathan

Theme: Friendship.

Preparation:
A piece of thin dowel from the technology room can represent the arrow which Jonathan uses as a signal to David. You may ask a small boy/girl to kneel a few metres away from you to represent the servant. At the appropriate moment throw the "arrow" beyond the servant who may retrieve it for you.

The Story:

David had grown into a handsome and strong young man. He still spent time looking after his father's sheep and, sometimes he would sit in the sunshine writing songs on his lyre (something like a small harp). News of his defeat of Goliath had spread far and wide and David had earned himself the reputation of being something of a great warrior.

Meanwhile King Saul went from bad to worse. He could not be relied upon to rule his country wisely. His moods would change without warning and even his servants were afraid to come near him in case he flew into one of his rages. His advisors and courtiers met secretly one day to discuss just what could be done.

"Perhaps there might be found a special herb which would sooth the king," suggested one.

"Maybe someone could read him a poem," said another.

"What about playing him some music to quieten his spirit?"

Everyone agreed that this last suggestion was a good one. But who was there who could play such music? One of the men said that he had heard a shepherd boy playing his lyre out on the hillside one day. It was agreed that this boy should be brought to the king immediately.

And so it was that David found himself in the court of King Saul. At first everything went well. If Saul became angry or irritable then David would be sent for and plucking the strings of his lyre he would play beautiful and peaceful music and the king would become peaceful again. But, one day, Saul was lying in his chamber when he was awoken from his sleep by a crowd singing outside his window. He sat up in bed and listened to the words of the song they sang.

"Saul has slain his thousands," they sang.

A smile came to the king's lips. They are singing about me, about what a great soldier I am, he thought to himself. But, no sooner had the smile appeared on his lips than he heard the next line of the song.

"...but David has slain his tens of thousands."

"What!" roared Saul, flinging the bedclothes onto the floor. Two servants came running hearing the noise.

"Quick, send for David," said one.

David arrived and began to play but he did not know that he was the cause of the king's anger. Saul was not to be quietened this time. He reached across to where a spear leant against the wall. In one movement he hurled it at David. Luckily David saw it coming and it smacked into the wood behind him with a quivering thud. Knowing that this was not the time to wait for answers David hurriedly left.

This happened on several occasions after and David began to think that he would be unable to remain in the king's court for much longer.

Now David had made a special friend while staying in the king's palace, Jonathan, the king's son. They would often go out hunting together, or practise with their bows and arrows or simply sit and talk together in the courtyard. In fact those who saw them together thought that they were so close that they were more like two brothers than friends.

"I am afraid that your father will lose his temper and do me harm," said David to his friend.

"I will talk to him," replied Jonathan. "I will try to find out how things are with him. For the time being I think you should go and hide nearby in the bushes. I will come out with my servant and give a signal. I will fire an arrow with my bow. If it lands before it reaches the servant boy, you will know it is safe to return to the king. If it goes beyond him, however, it means that you must leave quickly, for the king means to do you harm."

The two gave each other a hug for they both knew that they might not see each other again for a long time. David also knew that Jonathan was prepared to put his friend's safety above his own happiness.

David looked around. No one was looking so he crept into the nearby bushes where he could not be seen. He waited and waited. Time seemed to stand still but, eventually, Jonathan appeared. With him was his servant carrying a bow and a quiver of arrows. Jonathan took one arrow and loaded it into his bow. He beckoned to the boy to go ahead and stop. He then pulled his bowstring taught . . . and let fly. The arrow curved in a graceful arc . . . and then it fell . . . beyond where the servant waited. Jonathan motioned for the servant to collect the arrow. He looked up but could not see David. David had read the signal and knew he must leave immediately for his own safety. He knew that he may never see Jonathan again.

Prayer:

Dear God,

We thank you for our friends. For their kindness, for their loyalty, for being there when we need them. Help us also to be good friends to those around us.
Amen.

Follow Up:

What makes a good friend? List the qualities of a good friend. In the circle give each child in the group a slip of paper and a name of someone in the class. Each should write something good about the name on the paper. MAKE SURE NO ONE IS MISSED OUT. Do not accept negative responses. Shuffle the papers and read them all out.

One Bad Turn Deserves . . .

The Story of David and King Saul

Theme: Doing the right thing.

Preparation: *None*

The Story:

David had been in hiding from King Saul for many months now. Every so often the king's soldiers would come looking for some sign of David.

Even in the remote hills and woodlands, though, David's qualities as a leader could not be hidden. Tiring of the king's bad temper, many of Saul's soldiers left the palace and managed to find David themselves. Very soon David had a small band of loyal soldiers who would give their lives for him. The farmers and landowners who lived in that region were happy to have David's army nearby as protection from visiting, enemy troops. The farmers kept David and his men in food and supplies. Everything seemed to be going well until, one day, King Saul turned up.

It was one of David's soldiers who saw him. At first they could just see a cloud of dust in the distance, and then the glint of armour flashing in the sun, and then the clear outline of the men on horseback. At the front, in his full battledress, was the figure of Saul.

"Shall we prepare to fight?" asked the lookout.

"No," replied David. "Everyone find a hiding place as quickly as you can. It may be that Saul will pass by. He cannot know that we are here."

The men did as they were told. Nearby was a large cave and David and a number of his closest friends hid at the back and waited. Soon they heard the sound of approaching horses, their hooves sounding against the rock on the mountainside.

"Keep quiet and still," whispered David to his men. No one moved.

Then they could hear the soldiers dismounting and the rattle of their weapons as they put them on the ground. Perhaps they will stop for a rest and then move on, thought David. But then came the sound of a voice inside the cave entrance.

"I shall rest here a while. Guard the entrance and keep a watch for that dog David. I will kill him today if I lay my hands on him."

It was the voice of King Saul.

Then came the sound of footsteps, the rustle of a cloak, and then quiet. In a few moments there came the sound of someone snoring.

"Now's your chance," whispered one of David's men. "Saul is sleeping. You can take your sword and kill him while he sleeps. Then you can become king, and everyone will follow you."

David did not reply but he quietly rose to his feet and began to creep forward.

Nearer and nearer he crept and the sound of snoring grew louder. Now he could see the bulky shape of a man, wrapped in a cloak and lying in the entrance way. Closer and closer he came until he was near enough to reach out and touch the sleeping figure. Slowly he drew a small dagger from his belt. He held it briefly in the air for a moment, its blade glinting once in the light from the cave entrance and then, in one swift movement, he brought it down . . . and cut off a single piece of cloth from Saul's cloak.

Clutching both the cloth and the dagger David crept back to his hiding place.

Inside the cave it became very dark as night fell. In the morning, as the first cold light filtered into the cave, David heard the sound of the king getting to his feet and then voices could be heard outside.

"There's nothing for us here. Let's go on to the next valley and search there."

Then the sound of the horses snorting and the soldiers mounting up. David made his way softly to the entrance and looked out. The soldiers were already beginning to leave. After Saul had started down the steep slope of the mountain David leapt out of the cave and scrambled on to a rock.

"Saul," shouted David.

Saul spun around in his saddle. When he saw who it was he drew his sword and turned his horse to face back towards the figure standing above him.

"David!" shouted Saul. By this time all of Saul's men had turned their horses too.

"Look!" cried David and he held the piece of cloak high in the air.

Saul reached out and saw the clean cut of his royal cloth. Instantly he realised what had happened.

"David," called out Saul, dismounting from his horse. "You are a better man than I am. I have come here today to kill you, and yet you have chosen to spare my life."

"I shall not harm you. You are still the king," replied David.

"I shall not forget," said Saul, "that you have repaid me good for evil."

Prayer:

Dear God,

Thank you for the story of David who returned good for evil. May we learn to do the same.
Amen.

Follow Up:

Was David right to do what he did? Is it better to "get your own back?" What are the consequences for people who are continually trying to pay others back for hurting them?

Palaces and Prisons

STORIES OF RICH AND POOR AND OUR PLACE IN THE COMMUNITY

Heavenly Homes

The Emperor's Birthday

The Prisoners

The Magic Bowl

Not What We Deserve

Heavenly Homes

Theme: Giving to others.

Preparation: *None.*

The Story:

There was once a rich man who was well thought of in the grand city in which he lived. He regularly gave large sums of money to charity and he invited the rich and famous to his house often when he would auction one of his paintings, or something from his huge collection of antiques. The items were sold to the highest bidder, the rich and famous each wanting to show how wealthy and generous they all were, and the money raised was given to whichever charity was popular at the time. However much the rich man sold, there seemed to be no shortage of paintings or antiques to be sold another day. However many parties he threw there seemed to be no shortage of celebrities who loved to be seen at his parties, nor any shortage of purses to be opened for the next good cause that came along.

"You are indeed a good and generous man," sang the guests as they drank the finest wines and banqueted at the rich man's table. "You have spent so much money on entertaining us at your house. You have given generously from your own pocket. So many charities and good causes have benefited from your wealth."

"That is very kind of you to say so," replied the rich man. "It does me good to hear you say these things. I am happy to be of service to others and I am content to know that I will be rewarded in heaven one day for the things I have done."

One day the rich man was riding in his expensive car on the way to the opening of a new restaurant, when his driver took a wrong turning. Suddenly the surroundings changed. No longer were there bright lights and the bustle of shoppers in expensive coats. Instead the rich man, looking out of his car window, saw darkness and poverty and shuffling beggars. The houses, which could barely be called houses at all, were simply sheets of metal or wood leaning against each other, or nailed roughly into posts dug into the ground. The rich man watched as men, women and children in rags shuffled along dirty streets, or sat huddled in doorways or warmed their hands by crackling fires.

Just then his car stopped in a muddy rut in the road. Looking out of his window the rich man saw inside one of the doorways. There sitting on a simple mat of straw was an old woman. She was nibbling at a few crumbs of bread and sipping water from a wooden cup. There, on the floor beside her was a tiny mouse. As he watched, the old lady broke off some crumbs from her bread and put it before the mouse who quickly ate them up and began to wash his whiskers from the saucer of water on the floor.

"Does that woman not know that she could be spreading disease by feeding that mouse?" said the rich man to his driver. "How grateful I am that I am not like that woman."

Just at that moment the volcano which had been smoking gently for a thousand years suddenly exploded. Large rocks and molten lava spilled down upon rich and poor alike, falling upon the old woman's home and the rich man's car in an instant.

The rich man looked at the angel standing beside him and immediately knew that he was standing in heaven. At least I have led a good life and have given to charities and good causes, thought the rich man. I am sure to be rewarded for what I have done.

The angel said nothing but beckoned the man to follow him. As they went they passed great houses with huge golden gates and statues in the gardens. Rich curtains hung in the windows and a number of windows showed so many rooms it was impossible to count. But the angel did not stop there. They went on and on until they came to a place where the light shone less brightly. Here was a house, if it could be called a house, made by propping together a few metal sheets. Inside on the floor was a simple straw mat. It seemed to the rich man to be vaguely familiar.

"This is your house," said the angel.

"But there must be some mistake," said the rich man.

But the angel said nothing more and began to return upon the road they had come along a moment ago. The rich man chased after him. As they approached the place where he had marvelled at the most wonderful mansions he stopped in amazement. There, opening the door of the largest house, was the old lady he had watched that day. The angel was smiling at her and beckoning her into the house.

"But that is not fair," shouted the rich man. "I have given so much to others. Surely I deserve this house more than she!"

The angel turned and looked at the rich man.

"But it cost you little to give from all the wealth that you owned. This woman shared everything she had with any person or creature who came her way. We build houses in heaven from what we are given. This woman sent up the best materials!"

Prayer:

Dear God,

May we learn to give generously to others even if we have little ourselves.
Amen.

Follow Up:

Look in the Bible and other religious texts to see if there are any other stories and teachings on rich and poor. Rich people are often shown as mean in stories; is this fair or right? Do poor people always behave well? How should we judge how generous a person is?

The Emperor's Birthday

Theme: Playing our Part.

Preparation:

A large bowl, wooden spoon and a few jugs or empty wine bottles will serve to dramatise the telling of this story. As you relate the events of the birthday preparations indicate to children to come out and act the part of the villagers (simply pouring an imaginary liquid into the bowl is all that is required).

The Story:

It was nearly the Emperor's birthday.

Everyone was excited, especially the Emperor himself. Every year it had been the custom for the whole nation (for it was only a small country) to contribute something towards the Emperor's birthday present. This happened every year because the Emperor was good and kind and the people loved him dearly. But each year it became more difficult to decide just what would be a suitable present for such a special person. The Emperor's advisors and councillors met in secret to try to come up with an idea.

"Well, last year we bought the Emperor a dashing white horse to ride," said one.

"And the year before that we had a dove-cote built in his garden, with seven white doves."

"Yes, and they flew away if I remember!" answered the Chief Advisor to his royal highness.

"Well, how was I to know that they were really homing pigeons?"

"Never mind all that," cut in the Chief Butler. "What are we going to get this year?"

The advisors all began to pace up and down in the butler's large room.

"A new suit?"

"He has a hundred already!"

"Some white swans?"

"We're overrun with swans!"

"I know," shouted the Lord Chamberlain. "The finest wine ever tasted. That's what we'll give him."

"How are we to find such a wine?" asked the Head Cook.

"That's the point," replied the Chamberlain. "We don't have to. The people will bring the best from their wine cellars, we shall mix them together to make a blend the like of which has not been tasted anywhere for miles around."

"It's true," joined in the cook, "that our vineyards grow on the sunniest slopes and that our grapes are the most delicious you can find anywhere. I think it is a good idea."

And so it was that a royal proclamation was sent to every corner of the Empire, without the Emperor's knowledge, and every citizen was requested to find their choicest wine, their most delicious wine, their very best wine, and to bring it to the palace on the Emperor's birthday.

In every house from the smallest to the most grand each householder looked through their wine cellars, their cupboards and their outhouses to seek out the wine they would select especially for the Emperor.

The great day eventually arrived. There was great excitement as a long line of people, like a great snake wound its way along the road toward the Emperor's palace. One by one they filed into the great courtyard. Laid out on a huge table, upon a snowy white cloth, was a great silver bowl. It glinted in the bright sunlight as one by one the people filed up and emptied the contents of jugs, bottles and containers into the great container. First, a young man from the west of the country where the grapes grew red and ripe.

Then a lady from the coast where fine white grapes grew.

At the back of the line stood an old lady bent almost double with age.

She had been to her wine cellar and collected . . . an empty bottle.

"No one will know if I bring this one bottle of water from the well. There will be so much fine wine that my little contribution will make no difference."

She crept up to the bowl and quickly emptied the clear liquid into the bowl.

Two trumpets sounded and the time came for the Emperor to receive his gift from the people. He stepped up to the table and the cook handed him a silver ladle. He dipped the ladle into the bowl . . . and tasted. He licked his lips and dipped the ladle in again and again he tasted.

Turning to the crowd he spoke. "It's water, only water!" he said.

You see every man, woman and child had thought the same. My little contribution will make no difference. But, of course, it did.

Prayer:

Dear God,

When we are tempted to let someone else do the work, to tidy up the shelf, to get the books ready, whatever it may be; next time let it be me.
Amen.

Follow Up:

Think about the story. What mistake did the old lady make? Why did she think she could behave any differently to anyone else? When can you remember someone avoiding a task which resulted in more work for others (avoid direct criticisms of others in the group)? What rule, or principle, can you think of that might stop this happening?

The Prisoners

Theme: Working Together.

Preparation:
Have three or four handkerchiefs or pieces of cloth to hand. These can be produced at the relevant parts of the story to simulate the different escape attempts, rolling one, floating the next and finally knotting all of the handkerchiefs together.

The Story:

Across the seven hills of Ash-Ken-Benazi there stood a great prison. The prison was called Hash-Rehmah, which, in the language of the people of the long desert, means Place of Darkness.

The prison was home to nearly a hundred prisoners, all soldiers. They had been captured during one of many battles between the troops of Kazim-the-Terrible and the soldiers of Ivan-the-Unpleasant. Now Ivan's soldiers were cooped up in this dark prison with nothing to do but plan their escape.

But that was hopeless. For the prison was very high. Its towers seemed to reach up into the sky. There were no bars on the windows, as the walls of the prison were so steep and sheer that no one, save a madman, would dare attempt the climb, up or down. Below, on one side of the prison were great dark and jagged rocks; on the other rushed a torrent of white water fierce enough to drown anyone who was foolish enough to enter its waters.

One day there was an earthquake. Great cracks appeared in the walls of the prison but, miraculously, no one was injured. The prison guards of Kazim-the-Terrible were not cruel men, but they were terrified. They threw their hands up in terror and ran screaming out of the building, leaving the prisoners alone in their locked cells.

Everything became quiet. The dust settled. A single voice spoke.

"Brothers, we must find a way of escape. This prison will become our tomb if we do not."

"I hear you, Brother Wasim," came the reply from the next cell, "but you know there is no hope. The doors are locked and we have no key. There is nothing in our cell except a bed, our bed sheets and the wooden bowl for our food."

"We must lie here and accept our fate," said another voice. "Who knows? Perhaps the guards will return and free us."

They waited for one hour, and then two . . . and then a day and a night, but no one came.

"We cannot wait any longer. We must make our escape before the prison comes toppling about our ears." It was the voice of Wasim-the-Brave again. "I want every man who values his life to meet me on the ledge outside our window. Bring with you one bed sheet, wrap it around you for protection against the wind."

One by one the prisoners eased themselves carefully out of the open windows and stood looking down at the steep drop below. Soon there were nearly a hundred men standing on the narrow ledge.

"This is madness we can never escape this way. We shall all be killed!" cried one prisoner. And, straight away some of the men returned to the immediate safety of their cells.

"How are we to make our escape, Brother Wasim? The sides are steep and sheer and there are no handholds to help us climb down."

"I do not know yet, my brothers. But I do know that if we stay here we shall all eventually die. We shall starve to death or another earthquake may take us all."

"I have an idea," said a prisoner. "We could wrap ourselves in two or three sheets and they may protect us from harm if we jump. I shall try and you may all follow if my plan works."

"No, you will surely kill yourself," replied Wasim. "Here, let's wrap this wooden food bowl with a single sheet and see if you are right."

Wasim did as he had said and he hurled the bowl and its sheet into the wind. They all watched as the object fell toward the rocks. With a quiet thud, because the ground was so far away, the sheet hit the ground and split open showering the bowl in a thousand pieces.

"I have an idea," said another prisoner. "We can fashion wings out of the sheets and beat our arms. Then we may fly down like the bird."

"Wait," said Wasim, "let us make a man out of the wood from our bed and see if your plan will work."

So they made a man out of wood and strapped wings to him like a bird. They cast him from the ledge and, for a moment, he soared away from the prison walls. But, when only halfway down the descent he turned upside down and plunged towards the river where he disappeared quickly below the surface.

"There is another way," said a third prisoner. "If we make a sheet into a canopy it will hold the wind."

"Then let us try your idea with another wooden man. And so they did. Knotting the corners of the sheet they made a canopy for the wooden man. (They had made a parachute, but as parachutes had not been invented they did not know it.) The wooden man was launched into the air and for a time, he floated gently down. The prisoners cheered, but as he neared the bottom, the wind caught the canopy and the chute turned upside down, and the wooden man broke into bits on the rocks below.

The prisoners looked to Wasim.

"You have brought us to this ledge to die," said one man. "I prefer to die a peaceful death in my warm cell."

Another twenty men or so left those standing on the ledge and returned inside.

Then Wasim had an idea.

"Give me your sheet," he said to the man standing beside him. The man looked puzzled but did as he was told. Wasim took this sheet and knotted it together with his own. He motioned to others to do the same. In no time, all along the ledge prisoners joined their sheets together until they had a great, long, white rope. Soon other prisoners emerged again from their cells and added their sheets to the chain. Wasim then tied one end seven times around a bed which he jammed against a window. He then threw the end of the rope over the side of the prison. It nearly reached the ground.

One by one the men scrambled down the rope to safety. No sooner had they made their way onto the soft desert sand than another rumble brought the prison crashing down behind them.

Reflection:

Let us think about the story for a moment and reflect on its message. (Pause)

A task may be too great for one working alone, but many working together may achieve great things. May we attempt to help someone else today and in doing so make our world a better place to be.

Follow Up:

Think of as many examples as you can of team work for example, a football/netball team, fire-fighters, soldiers etc. Tell a story in the circle. Begin "Billie was part of the team but s/he wanted to play for her/himself . . ." Each person should add a sentence to the story showing how selfishness spoils teamwork. Discuss the ending. Suggest alternative endings etc.

The Magic Bowl

Based on a traditional Hindu story associated with the festival of Divali

Theme: Treating others fairly.

Preparation: *None.*

The Story:

There was once a man who lived with his wife in a small village. The man was very old and he was no longer able to work and, being too proud to sit at the gate and beg, he and his wife began to grow thin for want of a good meal. One day the old man decided that he would go to the temple to pray to the goddess, Parvati to ask for help. He set off in the early morning. It was a long journey by foot, and the old man, being weak with hunger did not arrive until late evening. Imagine his despair when he found the temple door shut. The old man slumped down upon the stone steps and fell asleep from exhaustion. It so happened that the goddess herself was inside the temple on this very day. She sensed that there was someone at the door who was in need of her help. She sent one of her attendants to bring in whoever was at the gate.

"But there will be no one there at this time of day," protested the servant.

"Go and see," said Parvati and, opening the door, the attendant found the old man sleeping. When he was brought into the temple the old man thought he must be dreaming but he gathered his thoughts enough to tell the goddess of his troubles. "Take this," said the beautiful vision. "It is a magic bowl and whenever you are hungry it will provide you with what you need."

The old man returned home to his wife and they enjoyed the richest food and drink on the table each day as they asked the bowl to provide dinner for them both. As the festival of Divali approached the old man decided that he must share his good fortune with others.

"Who better to share my good fortune with than the king himself," said the old man. "I shall set off at once and invite him to my house for a meal."
And so he did.

But when he arrived at the palace gate, dusty from the journey and poorly dressed, the guard would let him no further.

"Who do you think you are? And where do you think you are going?"

demanded the palace guard roughly. But the old man was not to be put off. He had been treated kindly by the goddess, Parvati, and he was going to share his good fortune with the king himself.

"I wish to invite the king to my house where I can provide for him a dinner better than anything he has ever tasted. The guard thought that this was a joke too good to miss, and he sent for the king's servant who told the king and, eventually, the old man was admitted to the royal chamber.

"Your most excellent majesty, I would be greatly honoured if you and your queen would do me the honour of dining at my humble house on the first night of The Festival of Lights."

"And what can you provide?" asked the king, hiding a smile of amusement from the little old man who bowed low in front of him.

"Accept my invitation your highness and you will see that I can give you the most delicious food the like of which you have never tasted in your life."

"Then I will come and see if what you say is true," replied the king.

But as the old man left the palace the king's servant gave him a warning. "If you cannot do what you have said then you will receive a beating for your trouble."

As the Feast of Divali drew near the king sent his servant to see what preparations were being made for the great day. The servant was astonished when, arriving at the simple house on the edge of the village, he found that nothing had been prepared at all for the king's arrival. Nevertheless, in a matter of days the king, his wife and other royal attendants and courtiers duly arrived and squeezed in to the little house. There the old man appeared and set an empty bowl upon the table.

"Wish for what ever you would like, your highness," said the old man.

The king looked about him. He did not want to be made to look foolish but he was curious to see just what kind of game the old man was playing. And to his astonishment no sooner had he spoken than the bowl was filled with all manner of delicious meats, spices, vegetables and fruits.

The king and his friends enjoyed every mouthful of the food served to them on simple wooden plates and there was so much that there was enough for the old man and his wife to enjoy when the meal was over. The king thanked the old man for his hospitality and promised to come again.

But, as the last of the guests were just leaving, the chief attendant returned to the room and snatched the bowl from in front of the old man and his wife.

"Please, do not take the bowl from us," begged the old man. "I am unable to work and my wife and I will starve without this precious gift."

"That is no concern of mine," replied the greedy servant, and with that he marched out of the door clutching the bowl tightly under his arm.

For the next few weeks the bowl would not produce any food for the wicked servant however much he shouted and cursed at it. Meanwhile, the man and his wife were again at the point of starvation and the old man decided once more to return to the temple. Again he journeyed all day and reached the steps of the temple after darkness had fallen. Again the beautiful goddess heard his prayers and had the old man brought before her. When she heard of the terrible thing that the servant had done she took a stick from the ground and instructed the old man to take it home and invite the king for a second time.

For a second time the old man made his invitation to the king and this time the king did not hesitate to come. All the courtiers and attendants sat watching as His Highness again asked for his favourite dishes to appear. Everyone was a little puzzled that, this time, there was no bowl upon the table, for none of them knew what the servant had done. Suddenly, as if from nowhere a large wooden stick appeared and began to beat the people seated around the table, even the king himself.

"Stop, stop," they cried.

"The stick wants its partner," shouted the old man. Without waiting for another whack from the stick the servant leapt up and ran all the way back to the palace. In no time at all he returned with the bowl and gave it to the old man. Soon everyone was enjoying the most wonderful dinner together.

No one ever tried to take the bowl away again. And the king came to dinner as often as he was invited, and he built a new home for the old man which he enjoyed for many years to come.

Follow Up:

Talk about the story. What punishment would you have given to the wicked servant in the story? What about the king? Was he guilty too? Think of examples of this sort of behaviour in school. How can we help people to behave more kindly to others?

Not What We Deserve

Theme: Undeserved kindness.

Preparation:

A piece of paper rolled like a scroll, or sealed in an envelope, will allow you to appear to read the letter from the Emperor at the end of the story.

The Story:

There was once an Emperor. His country was beautiful beyond comparison. The sun shone warmly upon green hills and valleys, the vineyards provided the finest wines, the orchards hung heavily with the ripest apples and oranges. There had been no war in the land for as long as anyone could remember, not in their father's time or their grandfather's time, nor even in their great-grandfather's time.

As the Emperor looked out over his land he was pleased to see a country in which every man was content, or so it seemed. For the Emperor himself was beset by a deep sadness. He knew that he was fortunate to be the Emperor of such a fine country but he was missing one thing. He had no son, no one to pass on the privilege of ruling this great nation.

One day the Emperor sent for his Lord High Chamberlain and gave instructions to search for a child who would be suitable to become the Emperor's adopted son.

"But who will be willing to give up a son?" began the Lord Chamberlain, "even for someone such as you."

The Emperor thought for a moment. "Perhaps someone who is so poor that they will see that I can offer the child a better life. Go and see what you can do."

In a small street in the far corner of the country lived an old woman. Her daughter and her good for nothing husband had gone, leaving her to bring up their only son. All day long the old woman complained to the boy as if it were his fault. All day long she reminded him of the trouble he had caused her.

"Fifteen hours a day I work to keep you in food and drink and clothing. And what do I get for my trouble. Here we live in this poor house with no pleasure at all, just work, work. You don't ever get what you deserve in this life."

This was one of her constant sayings and so the child grew up to believe that you would never get what you deserved in life.

Then, one day, a man dressed in fine clothing appeared at the door. He took no time to explain that he had come to seek one who would agree to become the Emperor's son by adoption. The old woman, seeing her chance to be free of her responsibility at last, lost no time in signing the papers.

And so it was that the child grew up in the palace of the Emperor. He wanted for nothing and he enjoyed every luxury, fine clothing and rich food beyond measure.

One day, on his eighteenth birthday, the Emperor said, "My Son, I am to go away to visit my cousin in a far country. I shall be gone for a year and will then return to you. Meanwhile you are to take my place and rule the land. Care for my vineyards and farms, rule the people fairly, and take care of the poor."

"I shall do as you say," replied the son.

The Emperor left but no sooner had he gone than the son invited his friends around for a lavish party. He believed that you never got what you deserved in life and so he set out to take everything he could. In the year that passed he let the vineyards run dry so that there was no wine in the cellar; he let the farms go to ruin because he would not pay the labourers, and he allowed the poor to starve so that many died.

The Emperor's advisors called a secret meeting and the Lord Chamberlain himself decided that enough was enough. The Emperor's son must be brought to justice before any more damage was done.

The courtroom was packed as rich and poor wanted to see what would be done with the man who had ruined their country in less than twelve months. Two of the best lawyers in the land spoke for, and against, the adopted son, and the most respected judge, after a week of consideration, gave his verdict.

"Young man," began the judge, "you have been given much within our land and you have chosen to spoil everything you have been entrusted with. You have both ruined the land and allowed the people to starve. This country reluctantly passes the sentence of twenty years in prison. After this I hope you will emerge a better man."

Just as the judge was about to bring down the hammer which showed that sentence had been passed, an official appeared and put a letter into the judge's hand. The judge opened it and read it aloud:

*"To the People from your Beloved Emperor:
I have heard of the things my adopted son has done and I am sad. For the wrong things he has done punishment must be made and I agree with any sentence that the land chooses to lay down. However, this is my adopted son and, therefore, I myself will stand in his place. I, the Emperor, will go to prison to pay for the injustice my son has caused. He shall go free."*

The judge looked at the young man.

"It seems," he said "that we do not always get what we deserve in life!"

Prayer:

Dear God,

May we appreciate those who show us kindness even when we do not always deserve it. Help us to do the same for others.
Amen.

Follow Up:

Divide the class/group in half. Ask them to write a character reference for the son in the story; one half should write one for the son before the court scene and the others for after he had been released. Was the son reliable, fair, honest etc. before he was tried? Do you think he would have changed as a result of the second chance he was given. Compare the two.

Class Lines

Ten class assemblies complete with presentations, poems, plays, stories etc. All ready to use, or adapt to suit your own class.

"Oh no! It's my turn to do assembly AGAIN!"
Here are ten off the peg assemblies designed to take the headache out of preparing The Class Assembly. Each assembly begins with a quick reference guide to resources and preparation required and links are shown with curriculum subjects. The age group given is only a guide but is drawn from the sort of topics often covered in those year groups. Every assembly comes complete with presentations, poetry, play scripts etc. although you may want to adapt some of the material to suit your own needs, get your class to write their own rap etc.

Class Lines

Mini Beasts

The Three Bears

Animals

The Weather

Keeping Healthy

The Ancient Greeks

Write On

School . . . Who Needs It?

Communication

The Ancient Egyptians

Mini Beasts

Age Group: 4-6

Curriculum Links: Literacy/Science/Citizenship

Resources:
Simple costumes for the play might be a red T-shirt for the ladybird, a yellow striped top for Harry Hornet; for the more adventurous wire and gauze wings and a card mask held on top of the head with elastic looks great. A large, green ball can represent the giant pea in the story.

Preparation:
Large pictures could be painted to show mini beasts/pets etc. The class need to learn the words and actions to Incy Wincy Spider.

The Assembly:

Narrator 1: Our assembly is all about mini beasts.

(The following can be read by the teacher and acted out by two children.)

One day Mum was cleaning the bath when she saw a big spider *(mimes fright)*. It was big and hairy and had eight legs.

"Help," screamed Mum. "I don't like spiders."

There was no one else in the house except her son, Ben.

"Ben," called out Mum, "there's a spider in the bath and I don't know what to do."

Ben was downstairs playing with his toy dinosaurs. When he heard Mum shout he came running up the stairs.

"What's the matter Mum?" he asked, "what's all the noise about?"

"There in the bath. A spider. Look," said Mum. She pointed.

"Where, I can't see it," replied Ben.

"There! Look!" Mum gave Ben a rolled up newspaper.

"Quick, hit it with a newspaper. Quick, before it gets away."

"Why?" said Ben. "It's not going to hurt you. It's more scared of us than we are of it."

Mum gave Ben a look. She did not believe him.

"I will catch it and put it out of the window," said Ben.

And so he did. Ben carefully cupped his two hands and gently picked up the spider. Mum watched but stood back.

"It won't hurt you, Mum. It's only little anyway."

Ben went to the open window and gently dropped the spider out. He watched as it uncurled, looked about him, and then scuttled away across the roof.

Narrator: Here is a rhyme about a spider, we have learnt together:

(Children say the poem with actions)

Class:
Incy Wincy Spider
Climbed up the spout *(fingers climbing up)*
Down came the rain and washed the spider out *(fingers flutter downwards)*
Out came the sun and dried up all the rain. (Open arms wide in an arc)
And Incy Wincy Spider
Climbed up the spout again. *(Fingers climbing up)*

Narrators:

There are so many little creatures in the world.

Some live in far away places.

Some, like the spider, might wander into a house for some warmth.

Many of them can be found in our back garden or in the school grounds.

Here are some of the mini beasts we have found out and about.

1.   Here is the ladybird.
      She is a member of the beetle family.
      Her wings are red with black spots and she has six legs.
      She lives on little green flies called aphids.
      Look for her on rose bushes in your garden.

2. Here is the butterfly.
    She has four brightly coloured wings.
    She begins her life as a caterpillar.
    She lays her eggs on nettles, or on a cabbage leaf.
    And grows into a beautiful butterfly.

3. Here is the snail.
    He has a grey body and no legs.
    He has two antennas to feel his way around.
    His house is a shell which he carries around on his back.
    As he slides along he leaves a silvery trail behind him.

4. Here is the bee.
    His body is striped yellow and black.
    He has four transparent wings which buzz when he flies.
    He collects yellow pollen to make honey.
    This helps the flowers to send the pollen to other flowers to make
    new seed.

5. Here is the spider.
    She has a round body and eight legs.
    She finds a dry place to make her home, in a shed or inside your house.
    She cleverly spins her web from a thread she makes in her body.
    She wraps her eggs in a silken sack to keep them safe.

Story:

(Six children act out the story as the teacher reads it aloud. A green ball will serve very well for a pea. Actors should stand in a line and pass the ball along, rather than actually throw it. Wally can pretend to poke the other actors to represent a sting.)

Narrator:
Here is a story about some mini beasts who had to learn to be good friends:

Once upon a garden there were five friends. (Each steps forward as his/her name is read.) There was Belinda Butterfly . . . Laura the Ladybird . . . Bertie Bumble Bee . . . Simon the Snail . . . and last of all Wally the Wasp.

They were all lying in the grass one hot summer day when a funny thing happened. Gemma, who was the girl who lived in the big house, was having dinner in the garden with her mummy. Gemma knocked a pea from her plate. She did not see it go. It rolled off the plate, across the table and fell all the way onto the grass. *(Place the green ball in front of the actors. A piece of cloth will stop it rolling).*

Belinda Butterfly, Laura the Ladybird, Bertie Bumble Bee, Simon the Snail, and Wally the Wasp all looked at the pea.

"What is it?" asked Wally.

"It's a small cabbage," said Belinda who had been born as a caterpillar on a cabbage plant.

"No it's not, it's a green stone," said Simon. "I crawl across stones every day."

"It looks the right colour for an aphid," said Laura the ladybird. "But I don't think I want to try and eat it."

"Well," said Bertie, "I think it's a ball."

"A ball?" said all the creatures together. "What's a ball?"

"I've seen Gemma playing in the garden with a ball," said Bertie. "We can all play catch with it. Look!"

And Bertie picked up the ball and threw it to Belinda. She caught it and threw it to Laura, who threw it to Simon, who threw it to Wally.
It hit Wally on the nose. Wally looked cross.

"What did you do that for?" he said. And with that he stung Simon on the arm.

"Ouch!" said Simon and he went away crying. *(Exits)*

The others looked upset, but they carried on playing the game.

Bertie picked up the ball again and threw it to Belinda. She caught it and threw it to Laura who threw it to Wally. Wally was not looking and it fell on the floor.

"What did you do that for?" he said. And with that he stung Laura.

It was Laura's turn to leave this time. And she did. *(Exits)*

The game began again.

Bertie picked up the ball and threw it to Belinda who, frightened of upsetting Wally again, threw it back to Bertie.

"What did you do that for?" said Wally. "It was my turn. You should have thrown it to me." And with that he stung Belinda. Belinda spread her beautiful wings and flew away.

"Throw the ball to me," said Wally.

Bertie looked at Wally. "No," he said, "I don't want to play anymore. You have hurt all my friends. I have a sting too, but I don't go around stinging people for no reason. I don't want to play with you anymore."

Wally picked up the ball and stood there on his own. "Come back," he said. "That's not fair. I can't play ball on my own. Come back and play."

Just then Samantha Spider came down on her silken thread.

"What's up Wally?" she asked.

"I've got no one to play with," said Wally. "They've all gone away."

"I'm not surprised," said Samantha. "You have not been kind to them. You stung them, and now they don't want to play with you any more."

"But I have no one to play with," moaned Wally.

"Well," said Samantha, looking stern, "you must learn to be kind to other insects if you want them to be your friends. If you like I will ask them to give you another chance."

And so she did. And Belinda Butterfly *(Enter in turn)* . . . Laura the Ladybird . . . Bertie Bumble Bee . . . and Simon the Snail . . . all came back to play.

And Wally learned how to be kind to other insects, how to play nicely, and how to be a good friend.

Can you be a good friend too?

Narrators:
Ben was kind to the spider that his Mum found in the bath.
We can be kind to small creatures.
Wally learned to be kind to his friends.
We can be kind to our friends, too.

Reflection:

Let's close our eyes and think about being kind to others.
We can be kind to small creatures by leaving them alone. We can provide homes for them by making special places in the garden for them to live. We can catch spiders in a cup when we find them in the bath.
We can be good friends to others by playing nicely, by not pushing on the playground, and by being kind.

Let us all try to be kind to others this week.

The Three Bears

An assembly based on the well known story

Age group: 4-6

Curriculum Links: Literacy/Numeracy/Citizenship

Resources:
Table, chairs and bowls for the story; beds can be small gym tables draped with a sheet.

Preparation:
Children can draw or paint pictures of the key items in the story. One child can play Goldilocks and mime the story as it is told. Lines that are chanted in the story will need some rehearsal.

The Assembly:

Narrator:
Today in our assembly we are going to tell you all about Goldilocks who went to a strange house and had a bit of a scare.

(In the following section children can hold up pictures as items are named)

Teacher: In our story there was one little girl.

Class: Her name was Goldilocks.

Teacher: In the bedroom there were three beds.

Class: One, two, three.

Teacher: Each bed had two pillows.

Class: Two, four, six. Three beds. Six pillows.

Teacher: On the table there were three bowls.

Class: One, two, three.

Teacher: Each bowl had three stripes.
Class: Three, six, nine. Three bowls. Nine stripes.

Teacher: In the story there were three chairs.

Class: One, two, three.

Teacher: Each chair had four legs.

Class: Four, eight, twelve. Three chairs. Twelve legs.

Class: One girl, three chairs, six pillows, nine stripes, twelve legs.

Teacher: What did we notice about these numbers?

Class: 1, 3, 6, 9, 12. We have learned to count in threes.

Teacher: And now we are going to tell you the story about Goldilocks and the Three Bears.
(Goldilocks and others take up their positions)

Once upon a time there was a girl called Goldilocks. Goldilocks liked to go and play in the forest although her mother had often warned her that it was not safe for a little girl to play there all by herself.

One day Goldilocks was picking flowers from the forest floor and she began to wander further and further from home. She came to a little path and she followed it along under the trees. Suddenly she stopped because, before her very eyes, she could see a little cottage. She was sure that she had never seen it before. It had two little windows, a bright red painted door and a little chimney at the top.

Goldilocks was curious as to who might live in such a house and so she walked quietly up to the door. There was no sound anywhere and so she turned the handle . . . and went inside.

There in front of her was a table and on the table were three bowls of porridge. One was very big, one was middle sized and one was so tiny it must have belonged to someone very small. Goldilocks tried the biggest bowl of porridge.

Class: But that was too hot!

Teacher: Next she tried the middle sized bowl of porridge.

Class: But that was too cold.

Teacher: Last of all she tried the smallest bowl of porridge.

Class: That was just right, and she ate it all up.

Teacher: Next she saw three chairs by the table. One was very big, one was middle sized and the third was very tiny so tiny it must have belonged to someone very small.

Goldilocks tried the first chair.

Class: It was too hard.

Teacher: Next she tried the middle sized chair.

Class: It was too soft.

Teacher: But then she tried the third chair.

Class: It was just right. But then the chair broke.

Teacher: Goldilocks looked at the broken chair but there was nothing she could do.

After eating the porridge Goldilocks was very tired. She saw some stairs and thought that there might be somewhere she could lie down and rest. She climbed the stairs and at the top she found a little bedroom. There were three beds. One was very big, the next was middle sized and the last was very tiny. So small it must have been for someone very small. She tried the biggest bed.

Class: That was too lumpy.

Teacher: She tried the middle sized bed.

Class: That was too soft.

Teacher: She tried the smallest bed.

Class: That was just right. And she fell fast asleep.

Teacher: Meanwhile the three bears who lived in the cottage had returned from their walk in the forest. They opened the door and went inside. They saw the empty bowls on the table.

Class: Who's been eating my porridge?

Teacher: Said Daddy Bear

Class: Who's been eating my porridge?

Teacher: Said Mummy Bear

Class: Who's been eating my porridge?

Teacher: Said Baby Bear…and she's eaten it all up. Then the three bears looked at the chairs in turn.

Class: Who's been sitting on my chair?

Teacher: Said Daddy Bear.

Class: Who's been sitting on my chair?

Teacher: Said Mummy Bear.

Class: Who's been sitting on my chair?

Teacher: Said Baby Bear…and she's broken it too! Then the three bears went upstairs to the bedroom.

Class: Who's been sleeping in my bed?

Teacher: Said Daddy Bear.

Class: Who's been sleeping in my bed?

Teacher: Said Mummy Bear.

Class: Who's been sleeping in my bed?

Teacher: Said Baby Bear…and she's still sleeping there now. The bears crept forward and looked at Goldilocks sleeping soundly in the little bed. Goldilocks woke up. She saw the three bears. She jumped out of bed and ran all the way home, and she never went back there again.

Do you think that Goldilocks was sensible to go to that strange house on her own?

Class: No.

Teacher: What do think her Mum said to her when she got home?

Children: Don't go to strange places on your own.
Tell your Mummy where you are.
Leave other people's things alone.
AND DON'T TALK TO STRANGE BEARS!

Prayer:

Dear God,

Thank you for all the people we can count on to look out for us. Help us to remember not to talk to strangers and to keep safe.
Amen.

Animals

Age group: Year 5-7

Curriculum Links: Literacy/Technology/Geography

Resources:
This might be an opportunity for puppet making, each child making a puppet to represent the animals in the poem. For the story a simple puppet can be made by using a paper plate for the lion and a paper cone for a "finger-mouse".

Preparation:
If you want to be original the class could write their own poem in The Literacy Hour (a line each) based on the author's poem, 'Animals, Animals'. Posters will need to be made bearing slogans such as 'Save the Whale'.

The Assembly:

Narrator 1:
We have been learning about all kinds of animals at home and in the world.

Narrator 2:
Many of them are in danger and we are going to tell you why.

Narrator 3:
We shall also tell you how we can care for animals everywhere.

(Class recite poem. Lines can be shared by different children in turn with 'Animals Animals' chanted by whole class together.)

ANIMALS, ANIMALS

Animals, animals, everywhere,
The lion in the jungle, the cat on the chair.
Animals, animals, big and small,
The towering giraffe and the spider on the wall.
Animals, animals, in every land,
The penguin on the ice-flow, and the cheetah on the plains.
Animals, animals, we love you,
At home, on the farm, or living in the zoo.
Animals, animals, need our care.
From the hamster in the cage, to great, grizzly bear.
Animals, animals, are living in fear,
As we destroy their homes. As they are hunted for their fur.
Animals, animals, we love to see you there,
But we must all remember that it is our job . . . to care.

Narrator 4:
> We have been learning all about animals.
> We have made puppets/pictures of some of them.
> Here are some of our favourites.

(Several children can show (pictures or puppets) and talk about their favourite using the form below)

> Here is a lioness
> She lives in Africa
> I like her sleek coat and velvet paws.

> Here is an elephant
> He lives in India
> I like his long trunk and swishy tail

> Here is the polar bear
> She lives in the frozen Artic
> See her thick white coat.

(Other items can be added depending on the animals made/drawn.)

Narrator 5:
We enjoy looking after our pets. They are always pleased to see us, they cheer us up when we feel sad and they help us to learn to care for others.

Here are some of our pets:
(Several children can show pictures of their pets)

> This is my hamster
> His name is . . . .
> He makes me laugh when he runs in his wheel.

> This is my dog
> His name is . . . .
> I like to take him for walks.

> Here is my cat
> Her name is . . . .
> She likes to sit on my warm lap.

Etc.

Narrator 6:
A Greek storyteller called Aesop told this story about a lion and a mouse.
(The teacher or narrators can read the story. Two children, or the whole class, can act it in pairs as lion and mouse using puppets as described above.)

The Lion and the Mouse

One day, a little mouse was scurrying through the jungle when she came upon a lion. The lion, seeing the mouse about to dart away, put out one great paw, and held the little mouse by its tale.

"Oh, please lion," said the mouse, looking up at the huge face above him, "please let me go. I am hardly a meal for a great creature like you."

"And why should I let you go, little mouse," said the lion. "Can you give me a reason?"

The little mouse thought hard. "Well," said the mouse, "I may be able to return your kindness one day, if you do not eat me."

The lion laughed, amused at the idea. "How could you, such a tiny creature ever be able to help me, the king of the jungle?" said the lion.

But he was amused at the idea and he decided to let the little mouse go after all.

The mouse thanked the lion and hurried away down the jungle path before the lion could change his mind.

No sooner had the mouse disappeared into the green undergrowth than the lion gave a loud roar of surprise. As he had turned to leave he stepped on a hunter's rope, bringing a net down on him. The harder he struggled the more tangled he became. The lion knew he was trapped.

Then, back along the jungle path, scurried the mouse.

"Keep still lion," she said. "You spared my life and now I can help you."

"How can you help me little mouse?" said the lion.

But, without another word, the mouse set about nibbling at the net with her strong teeth. In no time at all there was a large hole and the lion was able to escape.

The lion bent down and thanked the little mouse with one lick of his wet tongue.

"I did not think that you could help me, little mouse," said the lion. "But you have paid me back for sparing your life by saving mine."

So you see the mouse and the lion had both learned to care for one another.

Narrator 7:
There are many animals in the world that, like the lion in the story, are in danger. The stripy tiger is hunted for its fur, poachers kill elephants for their ivory tusks and seals are killed for their skin. Many animals across the world are threatened as large areas of rainforest are cut down each day destroying their homes and habitat.

We must all play our part in looking after the creatures of the world.

(Here some children may hold up posters bearing slogans such as SAVE THE WHALE, PROTECT THE TIGER, STOP DESTROYING THE RAINFOREST etc. This should not be rushed and may be accompanied by suitable music or in an attitude of reflective silence)

Prayer:

Dear God,

Thank You for the animals of the world.
Thank you for the majestic elephant, the stripy tiger and the graceful gazelle.
Thank you for our pets who are our friends.
May you help those in other parts of the world who work to protect endangered animals.
Help us to care for all animals.
Amen.

The Weather

Age group: Year 7-9

Curriculum Links: Science/Geography/R.E.

Resources:
A globe, tennis ball, large paper circle for earth, moon and sun.
A weather map and flip chart.
Desk, rainwear, goggles and snorkel.

Preparation:
Some rehearsal of the movement of the sun and moon will be necessary in addition to practising the actors for Noah's news.

The Assembly:

Introduction: For 2-6 readers:
Today's assembly is all the about the weather.
Have you ever noticed that grown ups are always talking about the weather?
Will it be sunny?
Will it be rainy?
Will it be cold?
Will it be warm?
But where does all our weather come from. Well, today we are going to tell you all about the weather. Where it comes from... how it is made...and how it affects us all.

Item 1:
(Using an inflatable globe, a tennis ball and a large, yellow paper-circle children can move around the assembly hall to demonstrate the movement of the earth etc.)

Readers:
This is our world: It is a great lump of rock spinning in space.
It rotates once every 24 hours. This makes night and day.

This is our moon. It orbits the earth. It takes 28 days to complete one orbit. This makes the months of the year.

This is the sun. The earth orbits the sun. It takes $365\frac{1}{4}$ days to travel around the sun. This makes one whole year.

This flag *(attach with fixing material)* is where we live. The earth is tilted on its axis. Not too much, not too little, just enough.

As the earth travels around the sun in its orbit we are tilted a little nearer the sun for part of the year...sometimes a little away from the sun for part of the year. This makes warmer times . . . and colder times . . . spring . . . summer . . . autumn . . . winter . . . the seasons.

Item 2:

(Children may indicate places on a globe or map while pictures may be shown illustrating climate conditions etc.)

Narrator:

Different parts of the world have different kinds of weather. The parts nearest to the equator, this imaginary line on the world, *(indicates on the globe)* have the hottest weather, whereas the North and South Poles *(indicates on the globe)* are the coldest parts. These are different weather patterns that we call climate. Here are just four of the different kinds of climates around the world.

Reader 1:

Here is a desert climate.
Much of North Africa and large areas of Australia is desert.
The most famous desert in the world is the Sahara.
It is very hot and dry in the desert.
There is very little water here.
Nothing much grows here.

Reader 2:

This is a tropical climate.
South American rainforests have a tropical climate.
So too does India and much of Africa.
A tropical climate has two seasons. One very wet, one dry.
Tropical climates produce open grasslands and thorny trees.
When the rains come they can be very destructive.

Reader 3:

The polar climate is very, very cold.
The North and South Poles are the coldest places on earth.
In winter it is dark most of the time.
The land is continually covered in snow and ice.
Almost nothing can grow here.

Reader 4:

Here is a coastal climate.
Britain and Western Europe enjoy a coastal climate.
It has four seasons; Spring, Summer, Autumn and Winter.
Many different kinds of plants grow here.
People enjoy the changes of the seasons which we see throughout the year.

Item 3:
(A simple model of the water cycle can be set up by children holding a card-board hill, a watering can and blue cloth/cellophane for the sea.)

Readers:

How do we get rain?

Rain has to come from somewhere.

It begins as water in the sea. *(Wave cloth for sea)*

It evaporates in the warm sun and becomes clouds in the sky. *(flutter fingers above sea)*

When the cold air reaches the clouds the water turns back into water.

It rains on the hillside below. *(watering can)*

The water trickles down the hillside in streams, and in rivers. *(flutter fingers down hillside).*

The river reaches the sea. *(wave cloth)*

The cycle begins again.

Narrator:

In many cultures across the world there are tales of a great flood that covered the earth many, many years ago. The Bible tells the story of Noah who survived such a flood. We wondered what it would have been like if the television cameras had been there to record the event.

Noah's News

(Scene: Newscaster seated at desk, weather girl by flip chart and outside broadcast reporter on opposite side holding an umbrella or wearing a rain-coat.)

Newscaster: This is Nyim Badawi and this is World News reporting events from around the globe. Torrential rain is sweeping across large parts of the eastern hemisphere. Sources say that global weather patterns have been running out of control for nearly a week now. There are reports of widespread flooding in major cities across the world. Works of art in some of the world's great art galleries and museums have had to be moved to upper stories. The world's major rivers have burst their banks and cattle and other livestock have been swept away causing millions of pounds of damage. Rescue agencies say they are unable to cope with the scale of the problem. Lifeboat stations have had to ignore hundreds of 999 calls and concentrate on the elderly, government officials and people with large wallets.

Let's go now to Laura Lee Preston in the weather studio.

Weather girl: Thank you, Nyim. Well the weather in the last twenty four hours has been much the same as it has been for nearly a week now. A ridge of high pressure building up in the east seems to have broadened to create awful conditions for everyone . . . unless you are a whale or a duck. Heavy rain has been the order of the day and there is no sign of any let up. Let's look at the world map.

Our latest satellite picture shows thick cloud covering the entire world, and we can expect further outbreaks of rain in the east, the west, the north and possibly the south. We can safely say that the weather prospects for the next 24 hours are rain . . . rain . . . and more rain. *(Puts rain clouds on map.)*

House owners are advised to move belongings and grannies to upstairs rooms. Drivers should take extreme caution and should not undertake journeys without the aid of a wet suit and flippers. Some experts are predicting that this appaling weather will be with us for another 30 days or more.

Newscaster: Thank you, Laura. Now we can go live to our outside broadcast team where Michael Bucket has news of someone who seems to have seen all this coming.

Reporter: Bouquet actually! Yes, that's right, Nyim, it seems that one man here, in what was until recently a desert region, had, astonishingly, been building a boat out here in the hot sands.

Newscaster: Out of what exactly?

Reporter: Gopher!

Newscaster: Bless you!

Reporter: No, gopher wood. He was making it out of gopher wood.

Newscaster: How did people react to this?

Reporter: Well, neighbours said that the man, whose name we gather is Noah, began to build his boat some weeks ago long before there was any rain at all.

Newscaster: What was the reaction to that?

Reporter: It seems that people said he was bonkers . . . mad . . . insane . . . round the twist . . . loop de loop . . .

Newscaster: We get the picture, Michael.

Reporter: Anyway when it began to rain the locals thought that perhaps Mr Noah was not such a bad chap and that he might have space on his cruise ship for one or two others.

Newscaster: Did he?

Reporter: No. It seems not. He is planning to take his family, and two of every kind of animal into this boat, called The Ark. It appears that God had warned the people of the world of this impending disaster and that they took no notice. They carried on with their evil behaviour as before. It seems that he had chosen Noah and his family to survive what was to be a worldwide flood. We have no more details at the moment but as soon as we have anything . . . *(Sound of reporter speaking into a glass of water.)*

Newscaster: *(puts hand to ear as if listening on headphones)* It seems that we have lost our outside link. But reports are now coming in that God has put a rainbow in the sky *(a rainbow can be put up on the OHP)*. It seems that God has promised never again to flood the earth. He says that there will always be seed time and harvest in the future. So good news for the people of the earth . . . and for farmers everywhere. Please listen out for our further update at ten. This is Nyim Badawi for world News at 5.45. Goodbye.
(Newscaster and weather girl leave in snorkels, rainwear etc.)

Prayer:

We thank you God for the seasons, for seed time and harvest, for the beauty of the changing trees in autumn and for the bright summer sun.

Thank you for the climate we enjoy. May we be willing to send aid to those across the world who face disasters through bad weather. Amen.

Keeping Healthy

Age group: Year 7-9

Curriculum Links: Science/P.E./Food Technology

Resources:
A plastic model skeleton.
Paper cut outs of internal organs e.g. the heart.
Items of food, a packet of pasta etc.
A stop watch.

Preparation:
Many of the props can be gathered for use in teaching sessions and used again in this assembly. The class will enjoy learning 'the rap' by heart, in Literacy or Music time (or composing their own!)

The Assembly:

Narrator: In our class we have been learning about keeping healthy. Let's meet two characters who have different ideas about keeping healthy.

(Author's note: These characters may either be boys or girls. This tricky decision is left for the teacher to decide!)

Narrator: Here is Sofa Sam. S/he likes to sit and watch TV, all day long. Her/His favourite food is burger and chips. Her/His only exercise is playing computer games.

Sam: My name's Sofa Sam. I like nothing better than to sit all day on the sofa with a plate of burger and chips, watching my favourite television programme. For a change I turn the TV off and practise my computer skills. Wow! *(Mimes computer game)* Another alien bites the dust!

Narrator: Meet Jumping Jo. S/he eats only healthy fruit and vegetables. S/he exercises five times a day and never stops to watch the television. S/he's far too busy playing football, netball, hockey, swimming, cycling or running.

Jo: Hi! I'm Jumping Jo *(looks across at Sam)*. You won't catch me eating burger and chips. I like nothing better than a day out playing five different sports and then home for a nice bowl of fruit and veg!

Sam: Yuk!!

Narrator: Well, it's all too easy to see who's the healthiest around here. Or is it? Let's go and see the professor to find out a bit more about keeping healthy.

Professor: Hello Emma, *(or pupil's name)* what can I do for you.

Narrator: Well I have two friends, Sam and Jo. One eats burgers and never leaves the armchair; the other is always out doing exercise and eats only vegetables and fruit. Can you help me to decide who is the healthiest?

Professor: It seems obvious doesn't it? But I think we need to look a bit more closely at how the body works to find the answer to your question. Let's go and find out what these children in class . . . have found out about the human body.

Item 1: The Skeleton:

Expert 1: This is the skeleton. Without it we would simply be a puddle of skin on the floor. The skeleton also protects other parts of our bodies. For example, the skull protects the brain in our head, and the rib cage keeps our vital organs safe inside our bodies. The skeleton needs calcium to grow and this can be provided by drinking milk.

Pupil: What about fizzy drinks or water?

Expert 1: Well, some fizzy drinks contain lots of sugar which is bad for your teeth. We should all drink plenty of water to keep healthy, but milk provides the minerals needed to build up our bones and teeth.

Pupil: So neither Sam or Jo drank milk, and both lose points for that.

Item 2: The Heart and Exercise:
(Expert 2 standing by another child jogging on the spot.)

Expert 2: Here is . . . *(insert name)* She is jogging on the spot for a minute. I am going to take her pulse when she has finished.

Pupil: Why is it important to know about the pulse rate?

Expert 2: Well, the heart is a muscle and it needs to be exercised like any other muscle. We do this by running or playing games, or any other exercise we enjoy. For grown ups not drinking too much alcohol, or avoiding smoking are important ways to look after your heart. Now . . . has finished running let's take her pulse rate. Let's see . . . 1,2,3, . . . 139,140,141,142.

Pupil: Is that good?

Expert 2: Pulse rate varies slightly from person to person. At rest it might be around 80 beats per minute and after exercise it may rise to anything from 100 to 150.

Pupil: So, exercising all the time will mean a healthy heart.

Expert 2: No, no! No-one should exercise all the time. It is just as important to rest as well. Rest, and especially the right amount of sleep, helps our bodies to 'recharge its batteries'. Too much exercise can be a bad thing as well as no exercise at all. Also high carbohydrate foods such as bread, pasta and potatoes can keep our energy levels up to enable us to exercise for longer.

Item 3: The Organs:

Expert 3: Let's look next at the organs inside the body.
(Paper cut-outs of the items can be taped or pinned in place on a child, or a picture, as each is mentioned.)
Inside our bodies are all sorts of important bits and pieces which all have an important part to play.

Here is the heart again. It is pumping blood around the body.
Here are the lungs. They enable us to breathe. Exercise keeps these organs in shape.

Here is the liver. The liver helps you live. It turns food into useful products and removes any bad things we do not want in our bodies.

Here is the stomach. This is where our food goes. It uses special juices to digest our food.

Here is the large intestine . . . and the small intestine. These transport the waste products from our bodies that we no longer need.

Pupil: What sort of diet is helpful for our internal organs?

Expert 3: All of these organs need a certain amount of fat to protect them. This means that we ought to have some fat in our diets. Butter, milk, cheese and cooking oil etc. all contain fats which do this important job.

Pupil: So eating no fat at all is bad for you?

Expert 3: That's right. Again too much or too little are both wrong. The secret is the right amount . . . a balanced diet.

Item 4: Healthy Eating:

Pupil: What are all these foods on the table for?

Expert 4: Well here are some examples of a balanced diet. Some protein to build up our bodies . . . *(holds up fish, meat, eggs, cheese)*

Some carbohydrate for energy . . . *(holds up bread, pasta, potatoes, sugar)*

Some fats . . . *(holds up margarine, butter, cheese, cooking oil)*

Some fruit and vegetables for fibre and those important vitamins; and milk for that healthy calcium for bones and teeth. And . . . don't forget to exercise and rest to keep your body in shape!

(Enter Professor and pupil again)

Professor: So you see neither Sam nor Jo are doing all of the things they should for a healthy lifestyle. Sam needs to eat less fatty foods but then Jo ought to eat a more balanced diet, including some fat. Sam must get some exercise but Jo should learn to rest as well as play, to help his/her body build up its reserves of energy.

Professor: Let's say our rap together to remind ourselves about being healthy!

HEALTHY LIVING RAP

Class: Keeping Healthy, That's the thing

           To make you move, to make you sing.

           Eating all the things you should

           Which means all diff'rent kinds of food.

           Meat and veg, fruit and fat

           We all need a bit of that

           Exercise helps us to grow

           And then some rest, so take it slow.

           Healthy Living, that's the key

           To being what you were meant to be.

           KEEP HEALTHY!

Prayer:

Dear God,

We thank you for our amazing bodies which can do so many things. We can see, hear, shout, sing, run, jump and play games. Help us to look after our bodies wisely, to eat well and to take the right amount of exercise.

Help us to appreciate what we have, and to be kind to those who cannot do all the things we can.
Amen.

The Ancient Greeks

Age group: Year 7-9

Curriculum Links: Literacy/History/Geography/P.E.

Resources:
Cards showing examples of Greek writing, word prefixes etc. Simple costume for the Greek gods, a mask for the Minotaur, or pictures may be drawn and copied onto acetate to illustrate the story as an alternative to acting out.

Preparation:
In a drama lesson children can rehearse miming athletic events in slow motion.

The Assembly:

Narrator 1: Welcome to our assembly all about Ancient Greece.

Narrator 2: Much of the way we live today has been affected by people who lived a very long time ago.

Narrator 3: The Ancient Greeks were very clever. They wrote fantastic stories, made wonderful buildings and developed a system of government that is in use all over the world today.

Narrator 4: Look. Here are just some of the things the Greeks did which we do today:

(Here children hold up cards with each word as it is spoken)

Readers:
Writing . . . the Greeks developed their own alphabet.

Stories . . . the Greeks told fantastic stories about strange creatures.

Science . . . an Ancient Greek called Demetrius worked out that everything was made up of small particles, which today we call atoms.

Democracy...today our system of government is based on Greek democracy. This means that anyone can have a say in how the country is run.

The Theatre . . . the Greeks wrote exciting plays and built lovely outdoor theatres to perform them in.

Architecture . . . the Greeks made beautiful buildings. Many of the styles they used have been copied in buildings down the centuries.

The Olympic Games . . . our modern Olympic games are based on the first Olympics held nearly three thousand years ago in Greece.

Education . . . children had different teachers for different subjects, much like a modern secondary school today.

Item 1:
(Here children may hold up first a map, and then pictures, or even 3D models they have made)

Reader: Here is a map showing Greece. Here is The Mediterranean Sea. Here is Athens, the capital of Greece. Thousands of holiday makers fly to Greece every year to sunbathe in the hot summer sun, or swim in the beautiful blue seas, or visit the famous buildings that have lasted for more than two thousand years.

Reader: Here is a Greek ship. It is made out of wood and has a large square sail. It was steered by two rudders at the back of the ship. The Greeks sailed to other countries to trade and sell wine, olive oil or pottery.

Reader: Here is The Parthenon. It was built on a hill in Athens, called the Acropolis. It was made in honour of the Greek goddess, Diana. Many believe that it was one of the most beautiful buildings ever made. Here you can see the great columns which supported the tiled roof.

Reader: Here is a Grecian pot. It was made by a craftsman called a potter. He would sit at a wheel which was turned by his apprentice, and he skilfully shaped the wet clay with his bare hands. The pots were decorated with wonderful pictures often showing warriors, musicians or the gods themselves.

Item 2:
(Letters and words can be held up on cards as they are said. 3D mathematical shapes could be made in maths/art lessons to show at the appropriate moment)

Reader: Here are some of the Greek letters of the alphabet. Alpha and Beta were the first two letters. From these we get our A and B. The word alphabet comes from joining together the words ALPHA and BETA.

Children learned to read and write by scratching their letters in a wax tablet with a wooden tool.

Reader: The New Testament in the Bible was first written in the Greek language. From the Greek word BIBLIO we get Bible.

Reader: Many of our modern English words today come originally from the Greek language.

ORCHESTRA   BIOLOGY   GEOGRAPHY   THEATRE

Words like:
DUO = 2, TREIS = 3, PENTE, = 5, HEX = 6, OCTO = 8, DECA = 10 . . .
. . . give us many of our mathematical words for shapes:

PENTAGON HEXAGON OCTOGON DECAGON DODECAHEDRON
. . . are all words taken from the Greek language.

Reader: Parts of words like:
POLY   MICRO   MEGA   TECHNE   PHONE
. . . again, come from Greek.

From these we can make words like: *(here have parts of words on card to show joining of prefix, for example, poly-gon)*
POLYGON (many-corners) MICROPHONE (meaning small voice) and MEGAPHONE (meaning big voice) TECHNOLOGY (meaning using skill)

Item 3:

Narrator: Here are some of the many Greek gods:
(Here pictures may be shown or children can be simply dressed and posed as the gods and goddesses)

Readers: The Greek people believed that the gods lived high above them on the top of Mount Olympus. There the gods were supposed to look down on the ordinary lives of the humans living below.

Reader: Zeus, King of the gods, god of the sky and the weather.

Reader: Hera was the wife of Zeus.

Reader: Ares the god of war.

Reader: Hermes was the messenger of the gods.

Reader: Athene was the goddess of art, wisdom and skill.

Reader: The goddess of love and beauty was called Aphrodite.

Reader: And Hades was the King of the Underworld.

Item 4:

Narrator: The Greeks told many fantastic stories about their gods. Here is one of them.

(This story can be shared between several readers and may be acted out by children. Alternatively the class may illustrate the story and project pictures on a screen by copying them on acetates.)

The Story:

Theseus and the Minotaur - *Based on the Greek Myth*

Once, long ago there lived, two kings.

King Minos ruled over the island of Crete and Aegeus was King of Athens. In time past, the people of Athens had killed the son of King Minos and, to punish them for this crime, the King of Crete plagued the Athenians with a terrible monster called the Minotaur. This creature was half bull, half man, and it lived in a winding maze below the King's palace at Knossos. Every year Aegeus had to send seven young men and women to the Minotaur to pay for the death of the King's son.

One day, Theseus, the son of King Aegeus, spoke to his father.

"Father, I cannot stand by and watch our people being destroyed each year," he said. "I will go and kill this evil creature."

His father pleaded with him not to go, but Theseus was a brave young man, and he could not be persuaded against the plan.

And so, when the time came for the seven men and women to go to sail to Knossos, Theseus was among them.

On arrival at the palace Theseus was placed in a stone cell to await the moment when he would face the Minotaur. As he lay quietly turning over in his mind how he might defeat the beast, there came a knock at the door. Into the cell came a beautiful, young woman. Her name was Ariadne and she was the daughter of King Minos.

"I have to come to help you," she said.

"But how shall I repay you for this kindness?" asked Theseus.

"Only by this, that you take me back to Athens to be your wife."

Theseus gladly agreed. In the morning the guards sent him into the maze alone.

"You'll never come out of there alive," they laughed.

Theseus made no reply.

As he made his way deeper and deeper into the long, dark tunnels he unravelled a ball of string that Ariadne had given to him. Then, turning a dark corner, he heard a sound of someone . . . or something . . . breathing. It was the sleeping Minotaur.

Theseus crept forward, and in a moment, stood next to the dark shape of the beast on the cold, stone floor.

Suddenly, with a great roar, the Minotaur leapt up and lunged at Theseus . . . but he was too quick for the creature. The young man leapt on the Minotaur's back and seized hold of its curved horns. The two struggled violently together and, after a fierce battle, Theseus stood up again . . . and the Minotaur lay dead.

Then, following the line of string the young prince made his way back to the cave entrance, and freedom.

Theseus returned to Athens to marry his new bride and, as they sailed away, there was a great earthquake causing the palace of Knossos to crumble and fall into ruin. The power of King Minos was no more.

Item 5:

The modern Olympics today is taken from the games held at Olympus thousands of years ago. The first Olympics were held in 776 BC.
Here are some of the sports that took place then . . . and are still part of the modern games today.

Can you recognise these sports?

(Here children individually or in small groups can mime each sport in turn, slow motion works very well for this activity. The narrator should give the answer after each one.)

RUNNING JUMPING JAVELIN DISCUS WRESTLING BOXING

The story of the first marathon is a very strange one indeed.

Reader: Greece was at war with Persia. The Persian army, led by King Darius landed at a place called Marathon. There, with huge numbers, they attacked the Greek army. It was clear that the Greek army would need help. A runner, by the name of Pheidippides, set off and ran all the way to Sparta for help. But the Spartans were busy holding a festival and said they could not come straight away. Poor Pheidippides ran all the way back to Marathon to tell the Athenian army the bad news. There, completely exhausted, he fell dead. The Athenians managed to win the day, but Pheidippides was not forgotten for his amazing effort.

Today the marathon race of 42 km is part of the Olympic Games but not everyone knows how it all began.

Narrator: The Greeks gave us many things from their culture.
Ariadne gave a ball of string to Theseus.
Pheidippides gave his life for his country.

Prayer:

Dear God,

We thank you for all those people who give to us in so many ways. Through the things we need, presents at special times, a word of advice, and an act of kindness, may we too learn to give to others today, and in the future.
Amen.

Write On

An assembly about the history of writing

Age Group: 9-11

Curriculum Links: Literacy/History/Art/R.E.

Resources:
A pen and a plastic/wooden sword. Children could make cards to show symbols, hieroglyphs etc. or these could be put onto acetate, or programmed into a multi-media production. (See Resources, page 183.)

Preparation:
Some work on the development of writing will need to be fed into lessons. There is an opportunity to make printing blocks from lino, shaping letters in matchsticks, string etc., and draw some decorated lettering from examples in books. In R.E. or Literacy you will need to read the book of Philemon in the New Testament and ask the children to write a (positive) reply.

The Assembly:

(The presenter begins the assembly and is interrupted by another pupil arriving)

Presenter: A long time ago someone said that the pen was mightier than the sword.

Pupil: *(appearing at the presenter's side).* What?

Presenter: Do you mind? I'm trying to introduce our assembly!

Pupil: Maybe! But you said the pen is bigger than a sword. Look here's a pen. Here's a sword. *(Holds up each item, weighing in his/her hands in a mocking way)*

Presenter: No I didn't.

Pupil: Didn't what?

Presenter: I didn't say the pen is bigger than the sword. It clearly isn't.

Pupil: Yes, you did. I was standing here when you said it.

Presenter: No. I said the pen is mightier than the sword.

Pupil: What's the difference?

Presenter: There's a lot of difference. The person who said it meant that battles can be won with the sword, or other weapons, but writing has the ability to change people's minds about things; perhaps whole countries might agree not to go to war because someone writes a letter to the King.

Pupil: Oh, I think I see.

Presenter: Well, I can't stand here talking to you all day. We're just about to do our assembly. Why don't you stay and listen. You might learn a bit more about how mighty the pen can be. (Both exit)

A Brief History of Writing:
(Children show examples of early writing drawn on cards/acetate slides/multi-media presentation)

Narrator 1: A long time ago when humans lived in caves and wore only animal skins, they wanted to communicate their ideas about their own experiences to others. They did this by drawing pictures of the animals they hunted and the places where they went. These simple pictures could have been linked together to make a simple message:

deer . . . sun . . . man . . . water . . . bow and arrow
(Arrange pictures in order.)

At daybreak (sun) . . . I am going (man) . . . by the river . . . to hunt deer . . . with my bow and arrow

Narrator 2: Five thousand years ago, the Ancient Egyptians were one of the earliest civilisations to use symbols to stand for words or sounds. This was one of the first forms of writing known to mankind. It was only quite recently that historians have worked out how to read these Egyptian symbols, known as hieroglyphics.

Narrator 3: Many of their symbols came from the things they saw around them:

water . . . a hand . . . reeds . . . a snake . . . a bird . . . a loaf of bread

Narrator 3: These symbols soon came to stand for sounds or letters, so that…
(Here example of Hieroglyphs can be shown and their letter sounds spoken)

Narrator 3: Here are some names of boys and girls written in hieroglyphics.
(Use hieroglyphics on individual cards to form the names of children in the class. Also include the names TUTANKHAMUN AND CLEOPATRA.)

Narrator 4: The Romans, who invaded Britain in the first century, brought their alphabet and numbers with them. The first Roman writing was often used for carving on temple walls and other buildings. To make the ends of the letters neat the masons added short cross-lines called serifs. You can still see this feature in use today in many printing fonts.

Narrator 5: Roman numbers were made up of single strokes for 1, 2, 3 and then other strokes were added to make a V for five and an X for ten. Four was made by putting a 1 in front of the V (5 take away 1) or a V and two ones meant seven. Roman numbers can still be seen today on old church clocks or as page numbers in reference books.

I II III IV V VI VII VIII IX X

Narrator 6: The alphabet we use today is really a mixture of a number of alphabets from civilisations of the past. The Egyptians, Romans and the Greeks too, all added letters, or changed the way an individual letter was drawn, until it became the 26 letters we know today. Here is how historians think we got our letter A.

(Class hold up cards to show development of the letter "A", see page 183)

(Class might sing the alphabet to one of the well known teaching tunes, chant it or make up a rap)

Narrator 7: Before the invention of printing, the first books had to be written by hand. In Britain during the period of history called the Middle Ages, monks copied out the Bible in the most beautiful handwriting. Each one took several years to write. The monks often began a page with a beautiful decorated letter. Here are some that we have made in our art lesson.

(Show examples of decorated lettering)

Narrator 8: Early printing was done by using wood blocks. Carving each letter by hand was a slow process but still better than writing by hand. It was not until 1440 that individual letters cast in metal were made. The letters could be moved to form new words, and they could be used over and over again. One of the first books to be printed by this method was Johann Gutenberg's Bible. It had 42 lines on each page and is still called the 42 line Bible today. We have tried printing letters by Lino cutting/string and matchsticks on card.

(Show example of printing and blocks used)

(Presenter and Pupil return)

Pupil: That's all very interesting but what about that stuff about pens and swords.

Presenter: Yes, yes, we're coming to that in a moment. But before that our class have been doing some writing of their own.

(Here several items of class work can be briefly read, shown etc. This may be examples of sentence building, story excerpts or poetry depending on work in progress at the time.)

Pupil: Yes, very good…but still no swords!

Presenter: I didn't promise you any swords did I? I just said that a pen could do more good than maybe a whole army of swords.

Pupil: What do mean?

Presenter: Well, we had a look in the Bible and we found this short letter from a man named Paul. He was writing to someone who was in the early Christian church. The man's name was Philemon. Philemon was very rich and had owned a slave called Onesimus *(O_nessy_mus)*. The slave had run away and Philemon was obviously very cross. Paul wrote to Philemon to try to help the two men make it up with each other. Here is what he wrote:

(The following is the author's paraphrase of the Book of Philemon based on the Good News Bible translation)

Reader:
Dear Philemon,

Greetings to you, and to all who meet at your church.

I pray for you always and I am so pleased to hear of all you are doing for the sake of the name of Jesus. Because of this I am going to ask you a big favour. I am writing on behalf of my friend Onesimus. He has come to me after running away from your house, and I know how cross you must be. In Greek his name, Onesimus, means useful. I hope that he will once again be useful to you. Although I would love to have him here with me, I am sending him back to you. I hope that you will be able to receive him back, not only as your slave, but as your friend.

If he has done you any wrong I, Paul, will pay you back out of my own pocket. Knowing you as I do, I am sure that you will be able to do this thing to please me, your dear friend.

I look forward to hearing from you soon.
Yours in Jesus Christ.
Paul

Pupil: What happened next?

Narrator: Well, we don't have Philemon's reply. That letter did not appear in the Bible. But what do you think? Here are some of the replies our class have written as they imagined what Philemon might have replied.

(Two or three reply letters may be read here.)

Pupil: I see what you mean, now! Philemon might not have been so kind if Paul had threatened him with a big sword. But, by writing a kind letter he persuaded Philemon to do the right thing.

Narrator: That's right. You see words, whether we say them or write them down can have a powerful effect on other people. Anyway that's all we have time for today. I'm off to write a letter to my Nan. She's not been feeling too well.

Pupil: That sounds a good idea. Perhaps it will cheer her up.
Narrator: I hope so. See you later, and don't forget your pen!

(Exit)

Prayer:

Dear God,

Thank you for the gift of language, of words and of writing. Thank you for the books we can read, and for the many opportunities we have to write ourselves. Help us to realise the power of words. Help us to not to use words to be cruel to others. Instead may we use what we say, or write, to encourage, to be kind, and to bring enjoyment to those around us.
Amen.

School . . . Who Needs It?

Age Group: 9-11

Curriculum Links: History/Music

Resources:
Victorian costume (optional). Lift up desks, although lifting desks can be mimed if not available.

Preparation:
Children need to be rehearsed with the Victorian rap and machine noises which might fit into music lessons.

The Assembly:

Scene: Several children are seated in a row to represent a class.

Teacher: Now everyone, I want you to turn off your laptops and take out your history books. Ben, what are you doing in your desk again? Now today we are going to find out about Victorian children. Do you think they had an easy life?

Sophie: No, Miss. They had to work down the mines and things like that.

Teacher: That's right, Sophie. And what else? John?

John: They had to get up early and go to the factory, Miss, and work the machines.

Teacher: Yes, they did

Jake: Did they go to school Miss?

Teacher: Well, it wasn't until much later in Queen Victoria's reign that people realised that children ought to have the chance to go to school. Many of them never learned to read or write or even spell their own name. Ben, are you listening to anything I'm saying?
(Pause while Ben continues to rummage in his desk)

Teacher: Ben, you're determined to blot your copy book today! You have until I count to ten to find your history book or you will have to stay in at playtime tomorrow.

132

Ben: *(To himself but aloud)* Oh, I hate school. Why do we have to go to school anyway? All you do is get told off. And what's a copy book anyway? I wouldn't mind being one of those Victorians. Never having to go to school.

Teacher: 1, 2, 3, 4, 5 . . . *(Teacher counts slowly to ten. While she does so Ben and modern children leave and are replaced by a Victorian teacher a girl (Emily) and other Victorian pupils.)*
Teacher: . . . 6, 7, 8, 9, 10. Have you not found your copy book, boy. You'll feel my cane if you've lost it!

Ben: What? Where am I?

Teacher: Are you asleep as well as stupid? Look there is your book. Now, dip your pen in the ink well and begin. The factory is the noblest of all Britain's industrial achievements. *(The children all begin to write. Ben looks around dazed.)*

Ben: *(whisper)* What's going on? Where am I?

Pupil 1: Your at St Winifred's School and you're about to get a clout if you don't start writing.

Ben: But I was just looking for my history book and now here I am.

Pupil 2: Keep your voice down. Old Jenks will give you a taste of his cane if you don't be quiet!

Teacher: Quiet! Stop talking and get on with your dictation. And make sure you don't blot your copy book, any of you!

Ben and Emily leave and the scenes are changed by each scenario coming on in turn. Emily acts as a guide in the same way that the Ghost in Dickens' Christmas Carol shows Scrooge his life. Children are arranged in a line to represent a factory machine. Other children enact operating the machine. Others are picking up fallen threads from below the workings.

Machine: *(with rhythm)*

GRIND	SHUDDER
WHEEZE	PULL
SHUTTLE	WHIZZ
CLATTER	CLATTER
RANG	RANG

(repeat over while lines are said)

Workers: Here we are. Working all day
Getting up early the factory way.
Here we are. Never we stop
Working all day until we drop.
Here we are pulling the threads
Machines are running go'nna cut off our heads!
Here we are running machines when we ought to be out fulfiling
our dreams.

Ben: What's going on?

Emily: Before there were any schools this is what most Victorian children had to do.

Ben: But what are those children doing?

Emily: They are picking up the threads that fall below the machines. They have to work long hours with hardly a break.

Ben: But they could have an accident.

Emily: Many of them do, but the factory owner can always find more children to work in their place.

Scene changes:
About a dozen children file on. They mime carrying coal, dragging heavy baskets and opening and shutting ventilation doors.

Miners: Here we are working away.
Working in the dark seeing no light of day.
Here we are. Working the mines.
Breathing in the coal dust, the muck and the grime.
Here we are working the coal dragging heavy baskets.
Look out below!
Here we are. Alone and afraid.
Letting in some air just so that we can be paid.

(Repeat in a whisper while Ben and Emily talk)

Ben: But they are only children . . . They shouldn't be doing this.

Emily: Thousands of women and children worked and died down the mines moving huge baskets of coal to fuel the new factories.

Ben: I don't want to see any more. Let's go.

134

Scene changes:
A rich house. Children are playing on the carpet.

Children: Here we are. Playing all day.
Mamma's in the parlour and Papa's away.
Here we are. In the nursery.
All these wooden toys are our play things.
Here we are wearing fine clothes.
All made at the factory where our money goes.
Here we are children of the grand.
We will never have to dirty our hands.

Ben: That's more like it. I wouldn't mind being like them.

(Enter chimney sweep and boy)

Sweep: Get up that chimney, it needs a good clean and my brush won't reach to the top.

Boy: But it's dark and I don't want to go.

Sweep: You hurry up or you won't have anything to eat tonight.

Ben: But that's not fair. Why should he have to go up the chimney when those children are allowed to play with toys.

Emily: They were born into a wealthy family. The boy was not.

Teacher: Look, you've made a large blot on your copy book. Out here at once. Six of the best for you. One, two, three . . .

(scene returns to the modern school)

Teacher: And that's the end of the history lesson for today. Put your books away everyone.

Ben: I never knew that children had to go to work like that in Victorian times. Perhaps school's not so bad after all. Now, where's my homework book gone?

Emily: Its there Ben. It's the one with the great big ink blot on it!

Prayer:

Dear God,

We thank you for our school and all the opportunities we have to learn. Help us to use them wisely.
Amen.

Communication

Age group: 9-11

Curriculum links: Literacy/Science/History

Resources:
Cards to show key dates in the time line, some musical instruments, a yoghurt-pot "telephone", an electric buzzer/or torch, and models of radios, televisions etc., made form cardboard boxes.

Preparation:
Research via the net, books etc. on the history of communication would provide the background for this assembly. Children could also find out about Morse Code and sign language for the deaf and be able to make simple messages in both. (See Resources, pages 181,182.)

The Assembly:

Introduction:

All: *(chanted/rapped/or sung)*

> Communication, Communication
>
> Communication, that's what you need.
>
> If you want to be the best.
>
> If you want to beat the rest.
>
> Communication's what you need!

Part 1:
Narrator 1: Communication. When we talk to our friends, when we show happiness by a smile, when we write something down, when we send a text message . . . these are all examples of communication.

Narrator 2: A great deal of communication relies on our ability to hear sounds. Sound is vibration. Sounds travel through the air to our ears where they are felt as vibrations in the part of our ear called the ear drum. Here are some examples of sound as vibration.

(Two or three demonstrations can be given with brief explanation by the children. Examples might be a twanged guitar string, a ruler vibrated on a desk top, some rice bouncing on a drum skin etc.)

137

Narrator 3: It is impossible to imagine living in a world where people do not communicate with one another. We are all communicators but we do not always communicate well. Let's listen to these people passing on a message. Have they really listened to what was being said?

(This piece can be performed in a line, each person receiving, turning and passing on the message to the next person in line.)

A: Thank Becky for the present.
She says she's ever so pleased with the blue pen.

B : Thank Becky for the present.
She says she's ever so pleased with blue again.

C: Thank Becky for being pleasant.
She says she's ever so pleased with blue again.

D: Thank Becky for being pleasant.
She says she's ever so pleased with blue again.

E: Tell Becky she's so pleasant.
She says she's ever so pleased with you again.

F: Tell Becky she's unpleasant.
She says she's never so pleased with you again.

G: Tell Becky she's unpleasant.
She says she never wants to please you again.

H: Tell Becky she's unpleasant.
She says she never wants to see you again.

(Becky joins the end of the line to receive the news!)

I: Becky, they say you're unpleasant and Jo never wants to see you again.

Becky: But she's my best friend! *(Leaves crying)*

Part 2:

Narrator 4: Nowadays we take communication for granted. We can send a text to a friend in seconds, watch television pictures from outer space, and, at the press of a computer key, we can link up with the World Wide Web for information.

(Class can construct a "human timeline" by holding up dates and pictures on cards)

Narrator 5: Here is a timeline of some of the great discoveries and inventions that have lead to the communications revolution we know today.

Reader 1: In 1821 Michael Farady was able to use the power of electricity to make the first motor. Without electric power it is impossible to imagine the invention of so many other machines that we take for granted today; the radio, television and the computer.

Reader 2: Amazingly, as early as 1832 a man called Charles Babbage made a huge machine which he called his "analytical engine". It filled several rooms and was made up of mechanical cogs and levers. It was able to carry out mathematical calculations and is thought of today as the first computer.

(A cardboard box model of a computer may be shown here)

Reader 3: The first message sent by a single wire was sent by Samuel Morse in 1832. The system of dots and dashes, which he called Morse Code, was used to send messages using a simple on/off switch. That is why we still see "telegraph" poles at the side of the road and not telephone poles.

(A simple demonstration using a torch or buzzer could follow)

Reader 4: Alexander Graham Bell was the inventor of the first telephone in 1876. In the early days of telephones you had to ask an operator to connect you to the line you wanted. Nowadays we are used to instant dialling, international calls and mobile phones.

(Two children could speak to each other using a yogurt pot and string telephone, explaining how the sound travels as vibration.)

Reader 5: An American, John Fassenden, sent the first voice message by radio in 1902. Four years later the first commercial radio broadcast began.

(picture of a radio can be shown here.)

Reader 6: In 1925 John Logie Baird was the first man to transmit a television picture. He placed the head of a ventriloquist dummy in front of his camera and the faint picture could be seen in the next room by his assistant. The first televisions only showed black and white pictures but nowadays we are used to colour televisions, videos and DVDs.

(Television made from a cardboard box can be shown here.)

Reader 7: The Internet began in the 1960s, as a system of communication between professors and computer experts in America. But it was not long before the World Wide Web became available to everyone in classrooms, offices and homes across the planet. We can connect to a site on the other side of the planet in seconds by plugging our computer into the telephone line.

Narrator 6: Of course, not everyone has the opportunity to listen to the radio, speak on the telephone or hear the voices on the television. Those who are unable to hear sounds are not able to share all those things which we take for granted. To communicate with each other deaf children learn a special sign language which stands for words and sounds rather than individual letters.

We have learned to use some sign language.

(Demonstration of a simple message in sign language. The message should be spoken after each word or phrase.)

Let's listen again to that message. Let's see if the children are better at listening this time.

A: Thank Becky for the present.
She says she's ever so pleased with the blue pen.

B: Thank Becky for the present.
She says she's ever so pleased with blue again.

C: With blue what?

B: The blue pen.

C: Oh, I see. (To D) Thank Becky for the present.
She says she's ever so pleased with the blue pen.

D: Did you say for being pleasant?

C: No, for the present.
She says she's ever so pleased with the blue pen.

D: Thank Becky for the present.
She says she's ever so pleased with the blue pen.

E: Did you say never so pleased?

D: No, ever so pleased.

E: Thank Becky for the present.
She says she's ever so pleased with the blue pen.

F: Thank Becky for the present.
She says she's ever so pleased with the blue pen.

G: Thank Becky for the present.
She says she's ever so pleased with the blue pen.

(Becky joins the end of the line to receive the news!)

H: Becky, Jo says thanks for the present.
She's ever so pleased with the blue pen.

Becky: Oh, great! I can't wait to see her again.

Narrator 7: So you see how important it is to be able to communicate well. Make sure you are good at speaking and listening today.

Hands together and eyes closed as we say a prayer about communicating.

Prayer:

Dear God,

We thank you for making us with one mouth to speak and two ears to listen.
Help us to listen to others, and to really hear what they say.
Amen.

The Ancient Egyptians

Age group: 8-11

Curriculum Links: History

Resources:
Costume *(not essential)* will add something to the atmosphere of this piece. Simple cloth "collars" can be made and decorated, and white cloth can be fastened to make Egyptian clothing.

Preparation:
It is helpful to have studied videos and looked at pictures of life in Ancient Egypt, especially as depicted in tomb paintings, models (shabti) and other artefacts. Preparation for use of this script may best be carried out by simple drama activities, you may ask all the children initially to experience "finding" an artefact, miming winnowing or dragging great stones etc. This works much better than telling children exactly what actions to do.

Performance Note:
If you have the space to "perform", this assembly works best in the round with the children seated at the edge of the hall. However, it can easily be adapted for the more traditional line of children at the front of the hall.

Back to Ancient Egypt
A PLAY FOR ASSEMBLY

(Two children enter the stage area where two people are carefully digging on their hands and knees)

Child 1: Hello, what are you doing?

1st Archaeologist: Oh! Hello. We're looking for something in the sand here.

2nd Archaeologist: We think that there is something buried here in the sand from long ago.

Child 2: It looks like hot work. What do you think you will find?

(Both children crouch beside the two workers).

1st Archaeologist: Look! Can you see that River over there. *(All look)* That's the River Nile. It has flowed there for thousands of years and the Ancient Egyptians made their homes on its banks.

2nd Archaeologist: They built their homes by the river because, every year, the Nile flooded and left rich black mud on its banks. This meant that there was good soil for growing things.

Child 1: Yes, but you still haven't told us what you are hoping to find.

1st Archaeologist: We were coming to that. You see the Egyptians who lived here three or four or even five thousand years ago, may have left something here in the sand.

2nd Archaeologist: Perhaps a ring or a brooch or a little statue.

Child 2: Look, there! There by your digger. There something poking out of the sand.

2nd Archaeologist: Here, take this little brush. Careful now. See if you can bring it out.

(The child brushes away the sand very carefully and holds up the object).

2nd Archaeologist: It is a little shabti.

Child 1: What's a shabti?

1st Archaeologist: A shabti is a little statue. The pharaoh who was like the King of Egypt would have little statues made of all those who worked for him. The Egyptians believed that the statues would come alive in the next world to serve the Pharaoh again.

Child 2: It sounds very strange and it all happened so long ago. How do we know all this really happened?

1st Archaeologist: Well, by finding objects like this and looking at pictures that were painted on the walls of buildings thousands of years ago.

2nd Archaeologist: Would you like to go and see?

Child 1 & 2: Yes please!

(All four characters walk to a hoop lying on the floor and step through it to signify going back in time. As they do so the rest of the class should enter in silence and strike up poses to represent the tomb painting, as farmers, builders etc. They keep as still as statues until "woken" by the vizier.)

Vizier: Greetings visitors to Egypt. I see that you have journeyed many days from a land beyond the Nile. What is your pleasure?

Child 1: Please Mr . . . er?

Vizier: My name is Atenmun. I am the lord high vizier of the Pharaoh Amenophis.

Child 1: We would like to see what life is like in your land, Mr Atenmun. That is if you do not mind.

Vizier: It will be a pleasure to show you the wonders of my lord's great land and its people. Follow closely behind me.

(Following the vizier the four look in wonder at the tomb painting. As each tableaux is arrived at it "comes to life" to show farming, or dancing girls etc. The following section can be adapted according to the tableaux you have chosen e.g. farmers, scribes etc.)

Vizier: Look, how the oxen pulls the plough to prepare the ground for planting.
See, here the people are planting the seed for the harvest.
Here the goats trample the seed into the ground.
When the wheat has grown it is cut with curved knives called sickles, and then the oxen trample the crop to break the grain from the stalk of the plant.

Child 1: What are those people doing?

Vizier: They are winnowing. The workers threw the grain into the air. The wind catches all the light chaff, the part that we do not need, and blows it away. The grain falls to the floor where we can collect it.
Now the workers gather the harvest into great baskets and carry it to the storehouse.

Child 1: The baskets are huge. They will never be able to eat it all.

Vizier: Ah! But the harvest must last until the following year. Who knows? The Nile may not flood next year and give us the rich soil for planting. Then we will have to rely on the crop we have in store.

1st Archaeologist: Look, I think you can guess what these women are doing.

Child 2: They seem to be dancing.

Vizier: Yes, they are dancing to entertain the Pharaoh.

Child 1: But what are those strange things on their head.

144

Vizier: They are combs of wax. They are filled with sweet smelling spices. As the girls dance before the Pharaoh, the wax begins to melt letting the sweet aroma of the spices into the air.

2nd Archaeologist: And I know who these people are. They are the scribes. They were very important in Ancient Egypt.

Vizier: You are right. Not everyone in Egypt learned to write. The scribes had to write down poems, stories and spells for use in the temple and in the Pharaoh's special buildings.

1st Archaeologist: The language they are writing in is called hieroglyphics. No one could work out what these strange symbols meant until quite recently.

Child 1: Can we go and see the buildings where they lived?

Vizier: We can do better than that. The Pharaoh is having his pyramid built. It is the tomb where he will be buried so that he can go over the sacred river to the next world.

Child 2: Wow! Look at all those people. There must be thousands of them.

Vizier: When the harvest is over everyone in the land is put to work to build Pharaoh's great monument. It will be greater than anything ever seen.

Look there are the masons cutting the stone.

Here are the architects and surveyors measuring and planning where each stone will be laid.

Here are the men who drag the stones on great sledges up this ramp to the very top.

Here the stones are laid in place and the masons come and cut and shape them to make a perfect fit.

(Enter Priest)

Priest: The ceremony of mummification is about to begin. Will you come and bring your guest with you, O, Atenmun, most high vizier to the Pharaoh.

Vizier: We shall come.

1st Archaeologist: *(to the children)* The Ancient Egyptians believed that you had to preserve the body after death so that it would be fit to take you into the next life.

Vizier: This way please.

(Children and Archaeologists take a seat to watch)

Vizier: Here the body of the Pharaoh is washed and cleaned.

Then all the internal organs are removed and stored in special jars.

Then the body is filled with spices and wrapped in long bandages.

The Pharaoh's body is then placed in a special case called a sarcophagus.

Child: *(stage whisper)* What happens then?

2nd Archaeologist: Well, the Egyptians believed that a special ceremony took place in the next world. The god Anubis, god of the dead would come and weigh your heart on special scales. If your heart was found to balance against a feather you could pass to the next world. Look!

Anubis: Hunifer, have you done no evil against your fellow man?

Voice of Hunifer: I have done no wrong against my fellow man, O, Anubis, Keeper of the dead.

Anubis: Hunifer, have your lips told lies against other men?

Voice of Hunifer: I have kept my lips from speaking lies against other men.

Anubis: Hunifer, have you harmed or taken the lives of other men unjustly?

Voice of Hunifer: Anubis, keeper of souls, I have not harmed or taken the lives of other men unjustly.

Anubis: Then weigh the heart in the scales of life.

(The scales swing and then are tipped in favour of the Pharaoh)

Anubis: The scales balance. Pass on into the next world.

1st Archaeologist: And I think it is time for us to return to our world.

Child 1: I think it must be way past our lunchtime!

Child 2: I don't think I feel hungry after that.

2nd Archaeologist: Thank you Vizier for your kindness in showing us all these wonderful things. We shall not forget them.

Vizier: I bid you farewell. May you have a safe journey to your world? May you keep safely all the things you find in the future that once belonged to us.

Archaeologist: We will.

(All depart through the hoop again. All the Egyptians exit. Looking round the children wave to someone)

Child 1: Look there's Mum.

Child 2: Thank you for taking us. Perhaps we can go again.

1st Archaeologist: I do not think that we can. But there are many books you can read to find out about people who lived long ago.

2nd Archaeologist: And there are museums which look after all the things that have been found from all those thousands of years ago. I wonder what people will say in a thousand years time about the things we leave behind.

Child 1: Oh No! I've dropped my computer game somewhere here in the sand.

Child 2: It's time to go. Perhaps someone will find it later. Come on.

(All exit)

Reflection:

(may be spoken by one of the characters, perhaps the vizier)

Let us be quiet for a time and think about what we have seen.

Many, many people have passed through the world in which we live. Too many people to number. Some of them were noble, some were bad, some were kind and good. May we, who live in the time which is now, learn the lessons from those who have gone before us.

May we be remembered in our time for doing what is good and right and true.

Depart in Peace.

Service Lines

Complete Services and Celebrations for Schools arranged in order as they occur in a school year.

Here are five services or celebrations for school arranged in (academic) calendar order. The services for Easter and Christmas may either be used in a place of worship or in the school hall. The activities provided for Pesach and Diwali are more likely to work better in a classroom setting. Special foods and crafts are provided to give something of the flavour of the celebration itself. This section closes with a leaver's service (or could be an assembly) to reflect on the importance of looking back and 'Moving On'.

Service Lines

Divali

A Christmas Gift

Pesach

New Life (Easter)

Leaving and Moving On

Divali

A classroom activity based on the Hindu festival of Divali

Theme: Celebration.

Notes:
The Festival of Divali takes place in the Hindu month of Ashwin, October or November in the western calendar. The word Divali means light. The activity provided here is based around the famous story of Rama and Sita from the Hindu epic story, The Ramayana. Of course many other deities and stories would normally feature in this festival (see The Magic Bowl page 86) which can last anything up to five days. It is only possible here to provide a taste of the actual celebration.

Preparation:
To capture something of the flavour of this colourful Hindu festival, more time will need to be spent on the decorations etc. associated with Divali with, than on the story activity itself, although this should form the centre piece. Colourful lights (divas), decorations and special foods can be made, easily absorbing craft lessons over several weeks, or a few days of concentrated activity in a special 'Divali' or 'Indian' week. Instructions for craft activities recipes etc. are printed below and further materials appear in the resources section of the book. (See pages 178-180.)

The Celebration:

The room is decorated with pandals, rangoli patterns adorn tables and walls, divas are available to be lit.

(Battery torches, fairy lights etc. will do as an alternative)

Leader: Let us celebrate Divali together.
Let us welcome the light of Divali.

Readers: Welcome to Divali
Celebrate together
Banish the darkness
Welcome the light
Let bonfires be lit in the forests.
Let fireworks light the skies above.
Watch as the light chases away the darkness.

Let the light chase away the darkness
As Rama chased away the wicked Ravana.
May the lights of the divas be lit,
Reminding us always of the light of
Divali.

(If available divas may now be lit, or lights switched on. A few seconds of quiet will add to the drama of the moment.)

All: Welcome Divali
Welcome Divali light
Let us celebrate together
The light has banished the darkness.

Now the story of Rama and Sita may be read with chosen children reading the parts of the characters as they arise, the teacher acting as storyteller.

Characters: The Story Teller   Bharata
Rama   Lakshmana
Sita   Ravana
The King   The King's Wife

The Story of Divali

Storyteller: There was once a King who had four sons. The eldest of these was his father's favourite. His name was Prince Rama.

The King also had three wives (it was the custom in those days for a man to have more than one wife). One of the wives had a son named Bharata. She was jealous of the popularity of Prince Rama and wanted her son to be the future king. She lay on her bed planning some way to get rid of the handsome and popular Rama.

Wife: I know a way to get rid of that proud prince once and for all. I remember that the king owes me a favour. He once promised me that I could ask him for anything and that he would grant my wish.

Storyteller: And so the king's wife left her room and went straight away to her husband. She found him lying on his royal couch and she approached him boldly. And this is what she said.

Wife: O Great King, my Husband, who has my devotion. Do you remember a promise that you made to me not so long ago?

King: And what promise was that? Remind me of it please so that I can do it.

Wife: You promised that you would grant me anything that I wish to ask for.

King: Then, if I have said this thing, I must keep my promise to you. What is it that you would ask for?

Wife: This, that you banish your son, Rama, from your palace for fourteen years.

Storyteller: At that the king fell on his knees and wept for he knew that he must fulfil the promise that he had made. And Prince Rama, because he obeyed his father in everything, agreed to leave the palace and go and live in the forest. With him went his beautiful wife, Sita, and his closest brother, Lakshmana.

Not long after this the old king died of a broken heart, and Bharata, knowing that Rama was really the rightful heir to the kingdom, went in search of Rama. When he found him he begged him to return.

Bharata: Rama, my brother and my friend. I know that my mother has done you wrong. Your father is dead and you are now our king. You must return and take your kingdom and all that belongs to you.

Rama: My brother, you speak kind words to me. But I cannot do as you ask. I have made a solemn promise in honour of my father. I have vowed to stay in the forest for fourteen years, and this is what I must do.

Bharata: Then I shall return with a heavy heart. The people will wait for you. Until then, goodbye, and safe keeping.

Rama: Goodbye. I shall return when my time has come.

Storyteller: And Rama and Sita lived happily in the forest for ten years. They made a shelter of bamboo and made friends with the animals of the forest. But they were not the only ones who lived there. In the forest dwelt many wicked demons. The fiercest of them all was Ravana. He had ten arms and ten heads. He saw Rama and Sita living happily in the forest and he made a plan to harm them.

Ravana: There is Prince Rama. See him walking in the forest with his beautiful wife, Sita. I shall take her away from him. Then we shall see what he can do.

Storyteller: Now Ravana knew that Rama was strong and that he would have to use his cunning; and so he sent one of his wicked followers into the forest disguised as a beautiful golden deer. When Sita saw it she immediately wanted it for her own.

Sita: Rama, Rama! See, there, a beautiful golden deer. Please go and fetch it for me. It would please me so much to have a pet of my own in this lonely forest.

Rama: Then you shall have it. Wait here by our cottage until I return.

Storyteller: And Rama raced off after the deer, and had soon disappeared from view in the dark forest.

Then, knowing that all was safe, Ravana set about capturing Sita. He spoke in Rama's voice to trick her.

Ravana: *(Spoken by Rama's actor)* Sita! Sita! I am here. Come to me my lovely wife.

Sita: That sounds like my husband, but something tells me that all is not well.

Lakshmana: Sita, I am here. Do not be afraid. See, I have put an enchanted circle about you to keep you safe.

Storyteller: But Ravana was cunning. He disguised himself as a beggar and came to Sita begging for food.

Ravana: Good day to you, pretty woman. Please can you spare some bread for an old beggar?

Sita: I would like to help you old man, but I am to stay here until my husband returns.

Ravana: But it will only be for a moment. Just step out here, and help me. I am so hungry and I can see that you have plenty.

Sita: Very well, but only for a moment.

Storyteller: But a moment was all that was needed. With a scream of surprise Sita realised too late that she had stepped out of the circle, and Ravana took hold of her hand and whisked her away in his chariot.

When Rama and Lakshmana returned Sita was gone.

Immediately the two realised that they had been tricked and, heartbroken, they began a long search. Their journey took them many miles through forests and across hills and mountains. On the way they were met by Hanuman, the monkey king; he had the gift of flight and he flew to find out where Sita was. Eventually he found her on a lonely island and in no time at all Rama, Lakshmana and the monkeys set about building a great bridge of rocks across the seas to the island where Sita was held.

There Ravana met them, and a great battle began. The fighting continued for hours but, eventually, Rama came face to face with Ravana. Drawing his bow he let fly an arrow but Ravana was too strong and the arrow fell harmlessly to the ground. Then, the gods gave Rama a special bow and with this he defeated Ravana and won the battle.

All: Hooray! Hooray, for Prince Rama!

Rama: I have come to rescue you, Sita, my wife.

Sita: I knew that you would come.

Rama: And thanks too to my friends the monkeys who have helped to defeat the followers of Ravana. Now we may return to our kingdom and be happy. And Bharata welcomed back his brother and Sita his bride. Flags and flowers were hung on every building and lamps were lit in houses to welcome home King Rama and Queen Sita.

All: Welcome Prince Rama.
       Welcome Queen Sita.
       Hang pandolas from the trees.
       Place divas at the windows.
       Welcome lights which banish darkness.
       Welcome Divali.

Ideas for Divali Decorations:

These items can be made leading up to, or following, the reading of the festival story. Or you can adapt your own ideas from the suggestions below.

Divali Lights:

These would traditionally be small oil lamps but here is a way to make a little divas that will be reasonably safe in a classroom setting. *(See also page 179.)*

You will need:
     modelling clay
     night lights
     paints and varnish
     sequins, braid etc.

1.   First take a piece of clay about the size of a golf ball. Roll it into a ball. Push a well in the middle with your thumb to make a pot.

2. Press the side thinner, turning as you go. Keep going until you can fit a nightlight inside.

3. Mould the pot into a shape, for example a heart or diamond. Use a knife or spatula to trim the top neatly. Roll a thin sausage of clay and join to the top edge of the pot by slightly wetting both edges.

4. When dry, paint your divas bright colours, varnish and decorate with braid, sequins and other sparkly materials.

Rangoli Patterns:

Traditionally floor patterns are made for the festival using a paste of rice flour, paint and water, or with dry powders. Find suitable designs on Indian prints or in books. Make templates and divide them into sections by tracing the lines in glue *(a squeezy bottle of PVA works very well for this)* and sprinkling on uncooked rice, lentils or other materials. Colours can then be added in the same way by carefully pouring in powder paints, or experimenting with food powders, grain products etc. A pattern is supplied in the resources section *(page 178)* or you may get the children to make their own based on a four sided symmetrical pattern.

Pandals and Paper Craft:

Garlands of flowers are draped around houses during Divali. Make your own by cutting out flower designs from tissue and hanging several on a piece of thread. Four or five threads can be hung vertically on a dowel rod, or twig, and hung from the ceiling.

A string of Indian elephants look great around the classroom wall. Provide a template, cut out, cover and decorate in Indian patterns with shiny foil. (A template for this activity appears on page 180.)

Divali cards are given during the festival and children can make their own. Buy some from the local shops to provide ideas.

Barphi:

Sweets are very popular with the children at Divali. Here is a simple recipe for Barphi, but adult supervision would be required for cooking.

Ingredients: *150g sugar*
                100ml water
                200g milk powder

1. Boil the sugar and water together for 6 or 7 minutes until the mixture begins to thicken.

2. Stir in the milk powder gradually. The result should be firm but pliable, like soft modelling clay in texture.

3. Turn into a flat, greased baking-tray. Pat and cut into shapes e.g. hearts, squares etc.

4. Decorate with edible silver balls and other colourful food items. Avoid nut products if any doubts about children with nut allergies.

Alternatively other cultural foods, such as samosas, may be found at the supermarket, or provided by parents for the occasion.

A Christmas Gift

A Christmas service for Primary School Children

Preparation:
Several presents with recognisable shapes need to be wrapped beforehand; readers need to practise etc. The poem would benefit from careful rehearsal and each child learning their line by heart if possible.

Note:
The term "leader" is used here being a general term designating a church minister of any denomination. Alternatively this role may be taken by the Headteacher or shared amongst several teachers. Narration, and possibly the story, may be read by chosen children from different classes.

The Service:

Welcome: by Service Leader

Narrator: We shall all sing our first carol, Once in Royal David's City

Carol: Once in Royal David's City *(Traditional)*

Item: ALL WRAPPED UP
Several presents with recognisable shapes are wrapped and can be held up in turn. This can be led by Minister/Service leader or shared amongst older KS2 children.

Leader: Christmas is an exciting time of the year. The High Street is busy with shoppers, lights are already hung on the Christmas tree and presents are wrapped ready for Christmas morning. Can you guess what each of these presents are?

Presents are held up in turn. The leader should act curiously, "I wonder what this one is!" etc. Hints and clues may be given. Each can be unwrapped in turn to reveal its identity.

Present ideas: A football
A violin
A book
A tennis racket
A baby doll

Narrator: Long ago a special gift was given to the world. It was God's gift at Christmas. In our special Christmas service we shall think about God's gift to the world. We shall now sing our next carol, Away in a Manger

Song: Away in a Manger *(Traditional)*

Narrator: Mary and Joseph were wandering the cold hillsides around Bethlehem. When they arrived in the overcrowded town, Mary was about to have her baby. But there was no room for them anywhere. A kindly Innkeeper gave them a gift . . . his stable, where Jesus was born and laid in a manger of straw.

Reading: The Birth of Jesus
            Luke 2 v 1-7

Narrator: Here is a poem about God's special Christmas Gift:
(This should be read by a class or group standing in a line. Each holds up the capital letter on card and says their line in turn, completing the whole alphabet by the end.)

Alphabet Incarnation

A king came, wrapped as a
Baby. Cradled in kindness.
Christmas Gift.
Down in a whisper of silence.
Earth his new home.
Fanfare of trumpets
Gloriously sounding.
Heaven watching
In angel expectation.
Journey of wise men,
Kings from afar for a
Long awaited
Messiah.
No crown he wore
Only swaddling and straw.
Proud parents
Quietly longing,
Responding to His cry.
Shepherds on cold hills
Travel to the tiny child.
Under starry,
Velvet skies.
We too may wonder;
eXcitement and awe. Our Baby King...
Yawning, in the manger lies,
Zzzz. Asleep in the stable.

Narration: We shall now sing: See Him Lying on a Bed of Straw.

Song: See Him Lying on a Bed of Straw by Michael Perry (Songs of Fellowship)

Reading: The Shepherds
             Luke 2 v8-16

Narrator: Christina Rossetti's lovely carol, In the Bleak Mid Winter, tells us of the gift of the shepherds and the wise men. If you had been there what would you have brought the Baby Jesus?

Reader: What can I bring Him?
             Poor as I am.
             If I were a shepherd
             I would bring a lamb.

Reader: If I were a Wise man
             I would do my part
             Yet what can I give Him?
             Give my heart.

             Let us sing it now:

Song: In the Bleak Mid Winter *(Traditional)*

Reading: The Wise Men visit Jesus:
             Matthew 2 v1-11

Narrator: We shall now sing, The First Nowell.

Song: The First Nowell. *(Traditional)*

Story: This story may be read by the leader or several children.

Sam's Present

Sam was sad. He so wanted to give his Mum the best Christmas present ever. But he had no money. His Dad did not have a job at the moment and his Mum worked evenings at the supermarket just so that there would be enough food in the fridge to last the week. They had been out to choose a Christmas tree, but only a small one, and Dad said that last year's decorations would have to do. Sam spent one wet afternoon, making paper chains out of the colour pages of magazines. It took him ages. When they were finished Dad helped him hang them up. They looked much more colourful than the ones you buy from the shop.

"They look great, Sam," said Mum.

But still Sam did not have any money to buy his Mum a present.

Jack at school had £5 a week pocket money. He was going to buy his mum a purse with embroidery on it. He had told Sam this in the playground in the last week before the Christmas holidays. Other children would buy china jugs, or a necklace, or a photo-album with FAMILY SNAPS written on the front in gold letters.

But Sam did not have any money to buy anything.

"Don't worry," said Mum, when she was doing the washing up one day. "I don't mind not having a present this year. Next year Dad will have a job and you will be able to buy me something nice then. You can make me a homemade card, with one of your lovely pictures on it. That would be great!"

But Sam did not think so.

He went up to his room and sat down on his bed. He was fed up.

Then he had an idea.

He would find something in his room that he really liked. He would give that to his Mum. It would be the best present ever.

He jumped down off the bed and opened his cupboard doors. In the bottom was a jumble of toy cars, some boxes of games, a few bits of jigsaw from a long forgotten puzzle.

What would his Mum like?

Then, there, right at the back, under a discarded chocolate wrapper he saw it.

His prize, championship conker!

He had beaten all the other conkers with it in the playground. And then, when the autumn had gone, he had put it in a box and cleaned it regularly with a bit of furniture polish so that it gleamed. He held it up to the light. It still gleamed and shone like a piece of dark jewellery. That is what he would give his Mum.

162

But it would need to be wrapped properly. He remembered that his dad had bought Mum a necklace once. It had been laid on a soft pad of cotton wool in a black box. Sam went and looked in the bathroom and found some cotton wool that his Mum used to clean her face in the mornings. He then looked around for a box. He could not find one. So he went down and opened the kitchen bin. There were not any boxes but there was a yoghurt pot. Sam took it out and washed it. He then went back up stairs and wrapped the pot in some red paper. He put the cotton wool inside and placed the conker lovingly inside.

On Christmas morning his Mum opened her present.

"Oh, it's lovely Sam," she said. "I shall put it on the window sill in the kitchen where I can look at it every day."

And she did. And when she did the washing up the water sometimes splashed inside the pot making the cotton wool damp. And the sun shone in through the window making the conker seed warm. And in the spring a little shoot appeared, and then a leaf . . .

. . . And now Sam is grown up. His friend's presents are hidden away in cupboards, or have been broken or lost. But Sam sits under the tree drinking coffee with his mum. And they are both sheltered by the branches of a beautiful chestnut tree.

Narrator: We shall now sing I Will Bring to You the Best Gift I Can Offer.

Song: I Will Bring to You the Best Gift I Can Offer *(Come and Praise)*

Reflection:

This can be read by several children or used as the basis for a short talk by the leader.

Sam gave his Mum a special gift. It did not look much. It was small and very ordinary. A conker. But it grew up to be something very special…a beautiful tree. A tree in which birds could make their nests; a tree to sit under and drink coffee and lemonade. A tree to spread its branches towards the sky, growing more splendid every day.

Jesus came into the world as a tiny baby. He was not dressed in the fine robes of a baby king. He was not born in a great palace or looked after by royal servants. He was born amongst the bustle of busy visitors to Bethlehem, born in a stable, laid in a manger. Apart from a few shepherds, and a group of travelling wise-men, almost no one knew he was there. Small. Unnoticed. Hardly enough to make the news.

But he grew up to be someone very special. He helped the poor, he healed the sick. He told people how to care for one another. He showed the world a glimpse of God.

Perhaps each one of us this Christmas can do something special for someone else. It may appear very small, not much, not worth writing about in the newspapers . . . giving a gift, a smile for the old lady who lives in your street, a word of kindness. But who knows just what good you can do, or what a difference each one of us can make.

Let us say a prayer for Christmas. Hands together and eyes closed.

A Prayer:

Dear Lord,

Thank you for Christmas time
For the lights on the tree, the colours in the shop windows,
For the excitement of opening presents.
Thank you for the story of Jesus:
For his birth in a stable,
For the visit of the shepherds,
For the gifts of the wise men.

May we learn the joy of giving at this special time of year.
Whether a present, a smile or in helping others.
May we know how to give the gift of kindness
This Christmas.
Amen.

Narrator: Let us sing together our final song, Light a Candle in the Window.

Song: Light a Candle in the Window. *(Come and Praise 2)*

Blessing or Close

Pesach

A classroom activity based on the Jewish Festival of Passover

Notes:

This re-enactment of The Festival of Passover might not be a suitable activity for a crowded assembly hall. As traditionally a simple family meal to recall the story of Moses leading the people of Israel out of Egypt, it would work far better as a class or group activity in the classroom.

Preparation:

The classroom may be set out simply for a meal with perhaps desks pushed together to make tables of 5 or 6. A tablecloth, tumblers, plastic cutlery, maybe even a lighted candle, will give the required impression. The items below can be easily gathered from most supermarkets. Write the four questions on cards for children to re-enact chosen moments in the story (this is usually done by the smallest boy in the household).

The Seder Plate: A lamb bone (not eaten during the meal)
A boiled egg
A green vegetable (parsley)
Bitter herbs (usually horse-radish)
Charoset (see recipe)
A cup of wine (use blackcurrant cordial)
Salt water

The Passover Meal

(The teacher should act as the head of the house and master of ceremonies.)

Teacher: We have come to this special night of nights to celebrate the Passover meal together. Let us drink together this cup of wine, symbol of joy, to remember what God has done.

1st Child: Why is this night different from other nights?

Teacher: Because we remember what God has done for us in bringing us out of a time of slavery in Egypt. And this special meal is a reminder of these things.

It all began nearly 4000 years ago. The people of Israel were made to work as slaves for the Pharaoh dragging great stones for the building of the pyramids. They worked hard and for many hours under the hot, desert sun.

2nd Child: What are these foods on the Seder plate? And what do they mean?

Teacher: This bitter herb is a reminder of the bitter times the people spent in Egypt. This Charoset resembles the mortar that they had to use to cement the stones together. The salt water is like the tears the Israelites wept.

But let's continue our story. At that time there was a man whose name was Moses. God spoke to him and called him to go to Pharaoh and ask that he might let the people of Israel go free. Shaking in his sandals, Moses approached the mighty King of Egypt.

"Please, O King," he trembled, "will you let my people go from this land?"

"How do you expect me to build my pyramids without slaves to carry stone? Your people cannot leave. Go away and do not bother me again," replied Pharaoh.

But Moses did not give up. He returned to Pharaoh again and again, and, each time Pharaoh sent him away. The Egyptians suffered a terrible plague. First the River Nile turned to blood. Then there were frogs everywhere, in the houses, the streets and in every barn and field. Then came flies and famine, spots and boils, locusts which ate every green shoot, and then days when the sun itself would not shine. The Israelites believed that God was showing Pharaoh that he must give way.

But still Pharaoh would not heed the warnings, and he refused to let the people go.

3rd Child: Is this lamb and this egg a reminder of something too?

Teacher: This reminds us of a time when our people offered gifts of food to God. This egg (here you may place the egg briefly above the candle) is like a gift of roasted meat. The lamb is a reminder of the sacrifice made to God at the last, and most terrible, plague. Pharaoh had enough warnings but refused to bend to God's wishes. The last plague saw the death of every first born in Egypt, including Pharaoh's own son. But the angel of death passed over the houses where the Jews had shared a meal of roast lamb and made a special sign on the doorposts of their houses.

4th child: And what is the reason for this matzot *(pronounced mot-soh)*? And why do we have this green vegetable on the Seder Plate?

Teacher: After this terrible night Pharaoh finally gave way. He gave permission for the people of Israel to leave at once. Gathering everything they could carry they left before the Pharaoh could change his mind. They did

166

not even have time for the bread in their ovens to rise *(show matzot)*. They hurried out of the towns into the desert. The green vegetable is a reminder that God cared for them and saw that they had food to eat.

And so we are happy to be together to remember these things on this special night. Let us drink of this cup again, and be happy for God's care for his people.

The Passover celebration would finish with the singing of songs together. A suitable song for this occasion might be Shalom Shalom (Come and Praise 2) which can be sung as a round (shalom means 'peace' in Hebrew). The head of the house would conclude by saying a blessing upon his family. The following may be said to finish this celebration if you think this would be suitable.

Blessing:

May the Lord bless you and keep you.

May the Lord lift up the light of His face upon you and give you peace.

Recipe for Charoset:

> 1 small apple
> grated chopped nuts
> walnuts
> almonds
> cinnamon
> a little red wine

Mix all the ingredients together into a rough paste. The result resembles the mortar that the children of Israel used in their time as slaves in Egypt.

Note:
Beware nut allergies.
It may be best not to invite children to taste this food item.

New Life (Easter)

An Easter service for Primary School Children

Preparation:
This service can be put together with the minimum of disruption to a busy timetable. The readings and prayers can be shared out so as not to overburden any one teacher or class. Children from the youngest classes might make the Easter pictures by painting, collage or arrange to bring in objects like a pot of daffodils, a toy lamb etc. The readings and play script may be more suited to the older children. Songs need to be practised in the few weeks leading up to the service, or you may have your own favourites which can be easily interchanged with those suggested.

The Play/Production Notes:
The short play script, The Stone Table, can be performed with minimum props and space. A table draped with a (grey) cloth and enough room for the actors to stand should suffice. Costume may simply be T-shirts and trousers/skirts, Aslan in yellow or brown and the girls in bright colours. The mice can be played by younger children wearing white T shirts. If desired a simple mask for Aslan can be made and the same for the mice, but this is not essential.

The Service

Welcome: By the Vicar/Minister/Headteacher.

Song: Lord of the Dance (Come and Praise)

Easter Pictures: A small group of children will hold up Easter pictures.
(The readings can be adapted according to the pictures/objects shown.)

Reader 1:   Springtime is here
Daffodils wave in the breeze
Showing new life

Reader 2:   Springtime is here
Catkins hang on the hedgerow
Signs of new life

Reader 3:   Springtime is here
New baby lambs skip in the fields
Bringing new life

Reader 4: Springtime is here
Fluffy chicks are hatched
Showing us new life

Reader 5: Easter is here
Easter Eggs are opened
Reminder of the Empty Tomb

Song: Now the Green Blade Rises *(Come and Praise 2)*

Reader 6: At Easter time we remember the death and Resurrection of Jesus. Having been put to death on a cross Jesus' body was laid in a stone tomb. Mary Magdalene, a friend of Jesus, went to the tomb to put sweet smelling spices on His body as was the custom then. When she arrived at the tomb this is what happened:

Four readers should now read this story as a dramatic reading from the Good News Bible or similar. One can act as narrator, reading the narrative in general, while the others take the parts of Jesus, the angel and Mary, reading only the lines spoken by these characters.

Reading: John Chapter 20 verses 1-18

Song: When Jesus Walked in Galilee *(Come and Praise)*

Play:

THE STONE TABLE:
A short play for up to 10 children based on the story, The Lion, the Witch and the Wardrobe by C.S Lewis.

Characters:	Aslan	4-6 Mice
	Lucy	Narrator
	Susan	

Scene: *Aslan is laying on the stone table. The two girls are nearby but suggest that they are watching from a little distance away.*

Narrator: In the story The Lion, the Witch and the Wardrobe by C.S Lewis, four children find themselves in the magical world of Narnia. There they meet Aslan the lion but their delight turns to sorrow when they see him put to death on the stone table at the hands of the White Witch.

(The two girls approach the stone table cautiously)

Susan: Look how he lies so peacefully now they have gone.

Lucy: The cowards! The White Witch and all her creatures, they wouldn't have done this without tying him up first.

Susan: But why! Why did he let them? He could have finished them all, finished them with one swipe of his paw.

Lucy: But he didn't did he? He simply let them. It was like he knew something they didn't.

Susan: I can't bear to see him like this.

Lucy: Oh! He's still wearing the muzzle. I wonder. Could we . . . could we take it off?

(The girls approach the body of Aslan from behind the table and mime removing the muzzle. Suddenly they both jump back)

Susan: Oh! Look, how horrid. There's something crawling all over him.

(Mice appear at the front of the table and mime nibbling at imaginary ropes around Aslan)

Lucy: Oh! What are they doing?

Susan: It's horrible. Get away. Get away from him. Why can't they leave him alone?

Lucy: Wait! Can't you see? Look what they're doing.

Susan: *(looking more closely)* But how strange. They are nibbling at the ropes that bind him.

Lucy: Yes they're friendly mice. But . . . poor little things . . . they don't realise that he's . . . *(Susan and Lucy look at each other)*

Susan: It's no use now. *(Looks up)* Look it's getting light now and it will soon be morning. *(Putting a hand on Lucy's shoulder)* There's nothing more we can do here.

Lucy: *(Shivers)* I'm cold.

Susan: Let's walk a little way. We can come back in a minute . . . and say goodbye.

(The two girls walk a wide circuit of the table, rubbing their arms against the cold. Mice slowly stand to conceal Aslan from the audience and Aslan and the mice together move to one side. Aslan should remain still and out of view. A loud crash is heard suggested by an instrument such as a drum.)

170

Lucy: What was that?

Susan: I don't know but I'm afraid to turn round and look. I'm afraid they are doing something worse to him.

Lucy: The stone table. It's empty. They've taken him.

Susan: Oh! Why couldn't they just leave him alone. Unless it's more magic.

Aslan: *(Stepping into view)* Yes! It is more magic.

Susan and Lucy: Aslan!

Susan: Is it you?

Lucy: Aren't you . . .

Aslan: It is me. Come and see for yourselves, children. I am alive.

Lucy: But you're not a . . . a ghost.

Aslan: *(laughing)* Do I look it?

(Lucy and Susan both run to him and each put a hand on his shoulder)

Susan: But what happened? What does it all mean?

Aslan: It means that, though the Witch knew the Deep Magic, she did not know that there was a magic that was deeper still, a magic that goes back before the dawn of time itself. If she had read what is written there she would have known this: that if someone who is innocent gives up his life willingly in return for another, then the stone table will crack and death itself will start working backwards. And now . . .

Lucy: Oh, yes Aslan.

Susan: What is it Aslan?

Aslan: I feel my strength returning to me. Children catch me if you can.

(Aslan runs. The girls chase him and all exit.)

(Following the presentation of the play would be a suitable place for a short talk if a vicar/ minister is present. Suggested theme: New Life.)

Song: Light up the Fire *(Come and Praise)*

Prayer:

Dear Lord,

We thank you for the signs of spring all around us.
For the new daffodils in the garden
For the baby lambs in the field and
For Easter Eggs in shiny wrappers.
All of which remind us of the promise of new life.
We thank you, too, for the story of Jesus and the Empty Tomb.
Help us to take those opportunities in our lives
To begin again for the better
To make our lives anew
Amen.

Song: The Servant King *by Graham Kendrick (Songs of Fellowship)*

Close/Blessing

Leaving and Moving On

A Leavers' Service or Assembly

Preparation:

Year Six children can spend some time in class selecting their favourite moments at primary school. Memories can range from first day at school to winning a sports trophy or sharing a special friendship. Contributions should be brief and need to be vetted for suitability (personal remarks about individual teachers are best avoided!) Children could write their responses in a sentence or two to read aloud from a card or learn by heart. They may paint a picture or bring in an item, say a school tie, to illustrate their contribution. Choose one or two children to play the parts of past pupils who will act as link presenters for the various items.

The Service/Assembly

Song: Travel On. *(Come and Praise)*

Scene: *Three pupils dressed as old people sit looking over old photograph albums. A coffee table or a standard lamp will give the impression of a lounge.*

1st Old Person: *(chuckles)* Just look at you in this photo. You're wearing your . . . school uniform. Very smart! I'd have hardly recognised you.

2nd Old Person: Let's have a look. Oh yes. You do look smart. Weren't you in that nice Mrs. . . . . class. I remember it well.

3rd Old Person: Yes it seems like only yesterday doesn't it?

1st Old Person: Yes, it certainly does. Good times though. They say school days are the best days of your life. Do you think that's true?

2nd Old Person: Maybe they were. I remember it all so clearly though. It's like I can see the people now. Like they're still here.

(The three bow their heads and several children from Year Six should read their memories of KS1. Each may begin "I remember when . . .)

1st Old Person: Yes, everything else seemed so big then, didn't it?

2nd Old Person: But we soon got used to everything. We made friends then that we kept all through school.

3rd Old Person: But going up to the juniors for the first time, do you remember that. It was almost like starting again, except that you still had your friends.

1st Old Person: Yes, I remember that too. Like it was only yesterday.

(The three bow their heads and another group should read their memories of the first two years of KS2. Each may begin "I remember when . . .)

2nd Old Person: And then we were big.

1st Old Person: We thought we were. It was like we knew everything.

3rd Old Person: We were at the top of the school. There was so much to do, play in the football/netball team, sing in the choir, do our exams.

(all groan)

1st Old Person: Before long it was time to go on to secondary school.

2nd Old Person: Yes, off to . . . . . . *(here some of the schools may be named).*

(The three bow their heads. A third group should read their memories of the last two years of KS2. Each may begin "I remember when . . .)

1st Old Person: Like only yesterday.

2nd Old Person: The best days of our lives.

3rd Old Person: I don't think I'll ever forget . . . School.

1st Old Person: Pass me that album. I've got more to stick in.

(Three bow their heads. Pause and Exit.)

Song: I Will Bring To You the Best Gift *(Come and Praise)*

A Prayer of Thanks:

Thank You God for all the opportunities we have known at
. . . . .School.
Thank you for all the friends we have made.
Thank you for all we have learned.
For all those who have taught us or helped us.
For all the memories we share.
Amen.

A Prayer about Moving On:

Father God,

As we begin a new chapter in our lives, as we move on to senior school, help us to remember all that we have gained here at . . . . . School. Help us to keep hold of those things we have learned, the skills we have acquired, the friends we have made. Most of all may we appreciate the people we have become.

Help us to settle in quickly, to make new friends and to make the best of the opportunities we will find in our new school.
Amen.

Song: The Journey of Life *(Come and Praise)*

Talk: by the Vicar/Minister/Headteacher

Song: One More Step (Come and Praise)

Close or Blessing

Resources

Rangoli Pattern

Copy this design to make a four-sided symmetrical pattern, or design your own.

The result can be decorated by sprinkling dry powders onto glued areas. Food materials are often used in traditional designs.

Divas

Indian Elephant

Use as a template for making a string of highly coloured elephants.

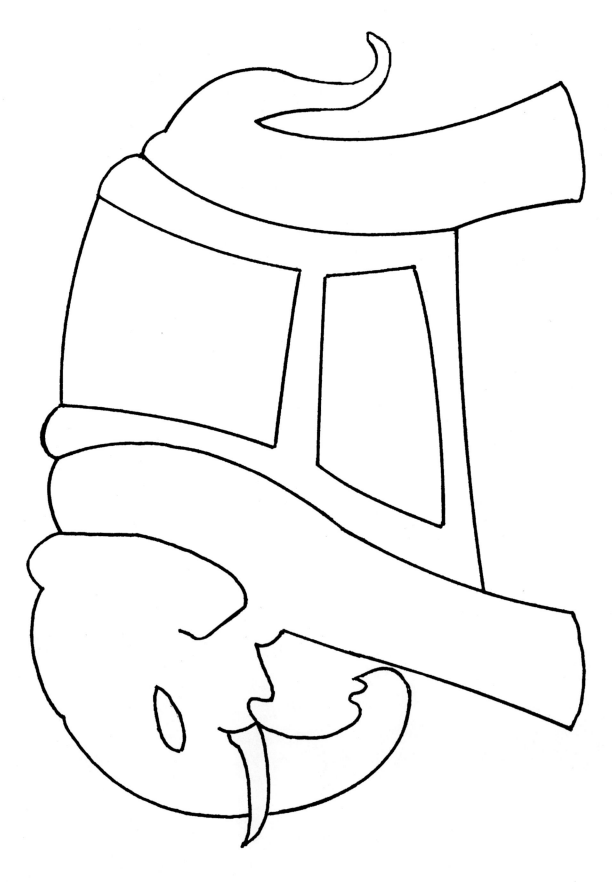

Morse Code Alphabet

A	.-	O	---	2	..---
B	-...	P	.--.	3	...--
C	-.-.	Q	--.-	4	....-
D	-..	R	.-.	5	.....
E	.	S	...	6	-....
F	..-.	T	-	7	--...
G	--.	U	..-	8	---..
H	....	V	...-	9	----.
I	..	W	.--	Fullstop	.-.-.-
J	.---	X	-..-	Comma	--..--
K	-.-	Y	-.---	Query	..--..
L	.-..	Z	--..		
M	--	0	-----		
N	-.	1	.----		

Sign Language

Standard Manual Alphabet as used by the Royal Institute for the Deaf.

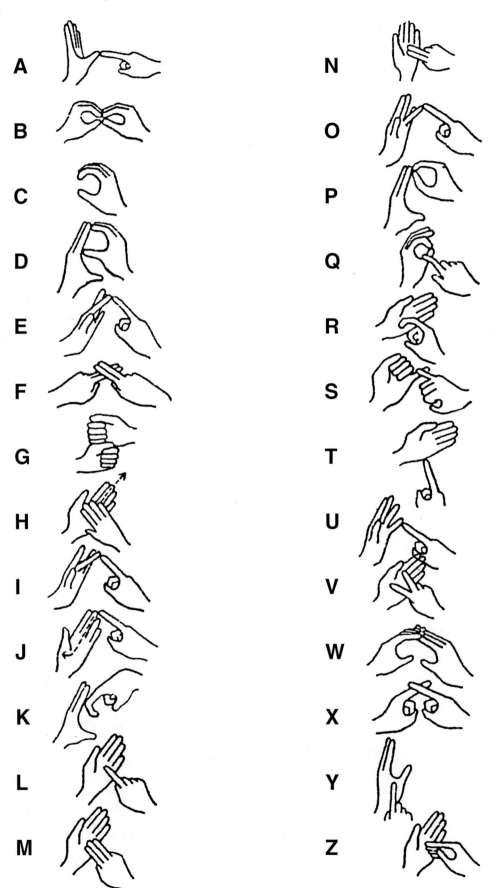

Hieroglyphics

A		vulture	**N**		water
B		leg	**O**		rope
C	or	basket/cloth	**P**		stool
D		hand	**Q**		hill
E		reed	**R**		mouth
F		viper	**S**		cloth
G		stand	**T**		loaf
H		rope	**U**		chick
I		reed	**V**		viper
J		serpent	**W**		chick
K		basket	**X**		basket cloth
L		lion	**Y**		reeds
M		owl	**Z**		bolt

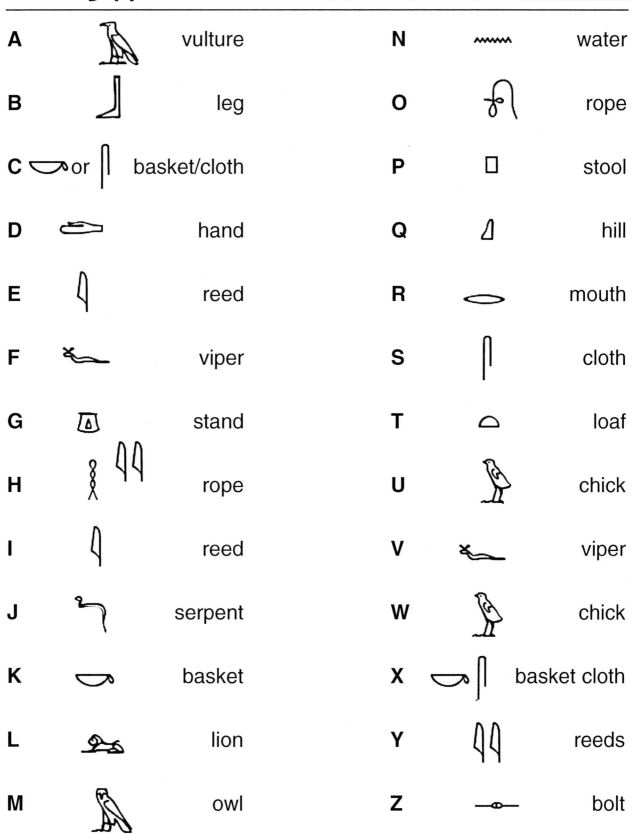

Development of the alphabet: the letter A.

  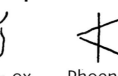

Egyptian   Seite aleph = ox   Phoencian   Greek alpha   Roman